AF240896

OUR COMMON CAUSE

Establishing the political power we lack

RIC: Citizen's initiative referendum
ETM: In all matters
ÉPNM: Written by ourselves

Étienne Chouard

OUR COMMON CAUSE
Establishing the political power we lack

Max Milo

Max Milo Editions, Paris, 2023
www.maxmilo.com
ISBN : 978-2-31501096-7

Acknowledgements

It is not easy for a neuron to thank all the neurons of a large collective brain that is growing at full speed and becoming aware of its power. It would be necessary to calm this daily press which is mine, to take time, to stop, and to thank, one by one, each human being who since fourteen years read me or heard me and understood, then helped to sow a little everywhere our seeds of ideas of freedom. Often this ally, without us ever having spoken, spontaneously, has also helped me a lot by defending me in a thousand forums and discussion threads where my work was attacked, distorted, slandered. I thank you all as best I can, those who are called "the nice democratic viruses" but who should rather be called "constituent citizens - white blood cells", immune defenses of the social body, as well as all those who do not recognize themselves under this flag but who nevertheless do the job well. We progress together, we grow together, we become political adults together. Without you, I would be nothing, it is simply obvious.

I would also like to thank my editor, who is very supportive and encouraging, and who helped me a lot to give birth to this paper child in the urgency of the news. I still have a thought for other editors, who also trust me, some of them for a long time, and who are patiently waiting for the time to bring to light with me their own constituent child.

I will save the most important for last. Thank you to my beloved children who have always helped me a lot. And of course, I thank my wife, a treasure of patience, intelligence and devotion, a beloved woman without whom I would never have succeeded in anything.

Preface

To tell the truth, I already knew the character, but from a distance.

I had taken the time to watch a few videos about him, in the context of the book I had just finished, *Délits d'élus*, and especially the one I was beginning to prepare, *Pilleurs d'État*. Étienne, I had also quickly gone through his constitutive theses and his Athenian discourse.

At the time, I found the character sympathetic but somewhat lunar, slightly offbeat. I saw him as a sympathetic Nimbus professor with a touch of madness, conveying with force and conviction slightly eccentric theses, coupled with a disarmingly naive unconsciousness that I didn't know if it was spontaneous or calculated. Nevertheless, instinctively, I liked the man, the character, because I had more or less understood that we were looking together for solutions to the growing malaise of the populations, that we felt each other coming.

Etienne, according to my personal analysis, was rather in the explanation of a future of ethics by the awakening of the collective and shared conscience while I was working in my own small way in the factual discovery, undoubtedly, of the sedation and the enslavement of the populations by a leading and unscrupulous minority. I still did not understand how all these "corrupt" elected officials, these corrupting "rich" people that I had referenced (with proof) had been able to corrupt the society in which we lived to such an extent and in such a short time. Without being on the same path, we were walking on parallel roads. Both of us found that the great book of democracy and liberties was more than well flayed by those who should have been its guarantors. We realized, each in our respective field, that the common book of our lives was written, drafted, conceived, truncated, abused, rewritten constantly by a few, and this, only (and more and more) to enslave and not to serve. We were thrown into a world and had to endure the language of profit while being led to believe that we were only reading a sharing script. A true swindle of life draped in a pseudo-democratic shroud.

I was there! We were moving forward with small, uncertain and clumsy steps.

Then one evening in September 2014 I truly discovered Étienne Chouard - a few minutes of true happiness! A real intellectual orgasm, enjoyable to the highest degree of the platonic and virtual seventh heaven by the simplicity of dialectical understanding that he will employ.

It is in the cathodic post. This evening he is invited in this program of polemists, *Ce soir ou jamais*, because for some years already, this one defray the chronicle and begins to frighten by making noise disturbing in the landerneau of the politically correct. He takes advantage of this to plough the soil of the intellectual certainties of the "right-thinking" with his controversial theories on "the ten serious reasons to oppose a dangerous text": the constitutional treaty. A crime that some people are beginning to find unforgivable because it could call into question, they say, the immutable basis (they also say) of our institutions.

I see a man in a white shirt, sitting shyly at the end of the couch, legs wisely crossed, a small notebook on his knees, hands flat or feverishly taking notes on the superfluous platitudes of some speakers like Attali, who is once again self-brushing by giving us lessons in life and democracy that he has always been quick to avoid applying to himself. Then, the presenter Frédéric Taddeï gives the floor to this guest from the end of the couch, teacher of law and economics in BTS at the Marcel-Pagnol high school in Marseille.

The camera starts with a tight shot, a substitute for an American shot, with the radiant face of Etienne Chouard who, in a smooth and penetrating voice, says only a few words. Simple words so true about our economic and political system that in one shot he fills the screen with his presence and charisma. We feel, we see that something is happening on the set. The reassuring appearance of a radiant country priest, with a calm voice, one of those voices that penetrate your soul, that breathes kindness, sharing and knowledge at the same time. There must have been a dozen guests on this set and instantly an almost religious silence sets in. The camera moves back a little for a wider shot and we see that all the heads are turned, motionless, attentive and silent at the same time, turned towards this man who speaks softly. The woman next to him (Coralie Delaume, a blogger by trade) steps back, as if to leave more room for the emerging grip of Etienne's words. In a fraction of a second, he fills the space with his charismatic presence and his penetrating words. Simple and true words that definitely challenge the mechanism of "democratic" submission that our institutions impose on us. A real treat for my eyes and ears.

That day, that moment, at that very moment, I told myself that we could win, that we would win. To choose rather than to suffer, to live and not to survive!

Since then, we have seen each other, seen each other again, understood each other, respected each other, listened to each other, and since then we have been walking together. We don't necessarily walk at the same pace and at the same rhythm. We don't necessarily have the same shoes, the same size. But we are on the same path of struggle, the same road of hope, the royal and ineluctable way that will lead us to more democracy and living together for all and not for the profit of a few.

I love this man (how can one not love him?), I love what he writes, I love what he says. I love what he lives and how he lives it. But, and this is important, I do not love him with the blind love of a bigot in need of a reference to his tasteless life. I am not in front of a guru, a master that we idolize whatever he does or whatever he says. For me, Etienne Chouard is a light among others that shines in the darkness of life, a palpable hope in the roughness of daily life, a sharing in the ocean of imposed individualism, a learning of living together in the respect of each one, a sower of beautiful seeds, those of freedom and choice not to undergo and that we must ourselves sow and water once taken in the hands.

I simply love his sincerity, the power of his words that speak to me, the immense tolerance that he radiates and that he lavishes, often naively, even towards those who most often (almost all the time) martyr him without even knowing him.

I was lucky to meet this man.

It is an honor for me to be able to put a few lines in the preface of his book.

It will be a pleasure for all of us to read it.

Philippe Pascot

1.
Our common cause:
to establish for ourselves the political power we lack

I have come to talk to you about democracy, the real one, the one that doesn't exist and that we really need today.

In 2005, on the occasion of a public debate in France, I wrote a ten-page paper on what revolted me in a so-called "constitution" that was proposed to the referendum, and I sent this document to my relatives and published it on my personal website. And there, everything changed for me... This tight argument for the no answered an expectation, a lack, and normal people sent it to all their contacts, everywhere in France and even in the world because they translated it into five or six languages... and thanks to Internet it became an event: when I came back from school, every day, after my classes, I opened my mailbox and there, a rain of mails started, every minute dozens of mails, all evening, all night... And for months, I tried to answer all these people, either people who relied on me, or people who said bad things about me. I was trying to "live up to it".

All the newspapers, radios, TVs came to my house to understand this phenomenon, the counter of my website was spinning like a fan, up to 40 000 visits per day (quite a peer-reviewed magazine, I can tell you...), 12 000 mails in two months ! Intense, warm, demanding mails too... And all this emotion stretched a spring in me (and it continues to stretch it today).

It is the gaze of others that has changed me, profoundly: the grateful and the suspicious gazes. My work is nourished by the importance I give to the gaze of others, and I recently discovered that men have known for a long time that it is important for the general interest: it is called *vergogne* and it pushes to virtue, it gives courage. For the Athenians, it was a foundation of the life of the city:

Plato: "Let the man who shows himself incapable of taking part in Vergogne and Justice be put to death as a scourge of the city" (Zeus' command in *Protagoras*, 322b-323a). And I think this is still an essential concept today: without going so far as to kill them, of course, *we should at least avoid at all costs giving any power to those among us who are shameless.*

So after the referendum, I continued, and I've been working like crazy since 2005, and here's why I'm working so hard:
- I seek to understand the main cause of social injustices,
- I discover the great ideas that founded the Athenian democracy (and many other democracies in the history of mankind, from the "primitive" societies to the pirate societies, through the medieval villages),
- I'm putting a lot of important words back in place,
- and I am thinking about good institutions that would protect us all from abuse of power in the long term.

I share this with all those who want to and we progress together, in permanent controversy. I am sometimes slandered or recuperated, of course, but it's not that serious. Anyway,

I absolutely need my opponents to progress. So, I do my best, I move forward, I look for it.

My method of searching is that of Hippocrates, perhaps the best idea in the world :-) This doctor said: *look for the cause of the causes.*

In other words, in order to cure an evil, to solve a problem, it is useless to attack the consequences, of course, but it is useless to attack even the various causes (since everything is multifactorial): there is always a determining cause (not the only one, but one that determines all the others): it is this one that we need, it is this one that we need to look for, it will be able to become *our common cause.*

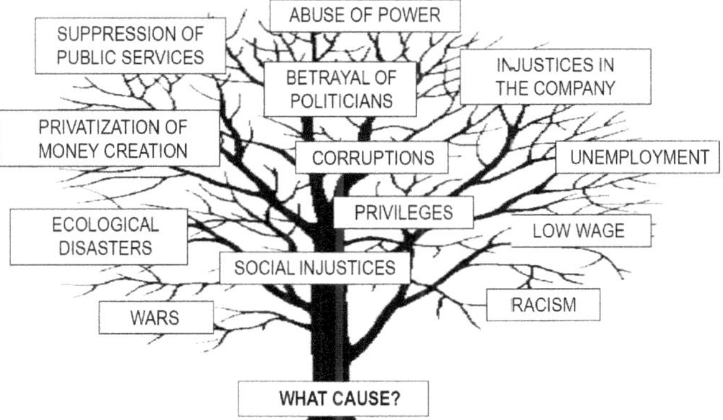

I of course share the struggle of my fellow resistance fighters (I made you a diagram to represent the tree of injustices and our specialized struggles), but I observe that activists are all fighting consequences:

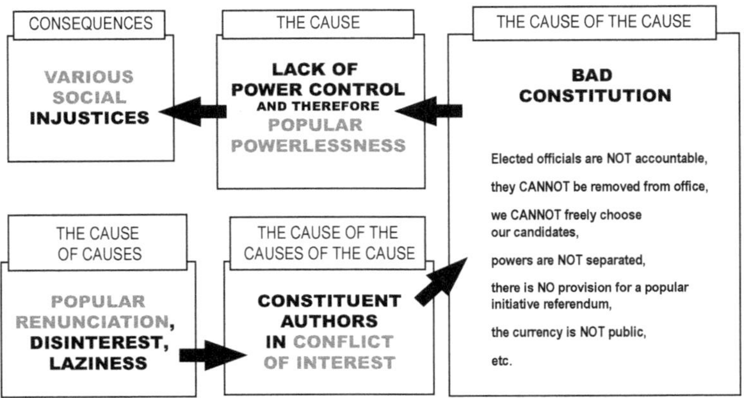

I observe that none of them takes the evil at the root: for me, the question I ask myself is "what makes all these horrors (ecological, economic, social...) possible?" That's what we need to understand.

I believe that what makes social injustices possible is the political impotence of good people, of normal people: if the people had the power to resist, they would do so, victoriously.

But then, this popular impotence, where does it come from? (I am still looking for the cause of the cause). It does not fall from the sky, our impotence: it is programmed, in a superior text... An essential text that nobody cares about! and which is called the Constitution. (Nobody cares about it, except the multinationals and the banks, note... the European constitution is the constitution of the banks.)

- It is in the constitution that elected officials are NOT accountable,

- It is in the constitution that they are NOT revocable at any time,

- It is in the constitution that we are NOT free to choose our candidates,
- It is in the constitution that the wealthiest are NOT prohibited from helping their candidates,
- It is in the constitution that the powers are NOT separate, not independent,
- It is in the constitution that the richest people are NOT prohibited from buying the country's newspapers,
- It is in the constitution that the RIC, referendum of citizen initiative, is NOT foreseen,
- It is in the constitution that money is NOT public,
- It is in the constitution that the people are absent and have NO power,
- etc.

But it is not finished, we must continue to search: this cause itself, this bad constitution, has a *primary* cause: **who wrote this text?** What is it that makes that, everywhere in the world, at all times, all constitutions program the impotence of the people? It is surely not a conspiracy: not everywhere, not all the time, it is not possible... No, this universal process has a universal first cause: according to me, all the human beings of the world, by laziness, by fear or by ignorance, give up writing their constitution themselves and all accept that it is professionals of the politics (parliamentarians, judges, ministers, members of parties...) who write and modify the constitution. *It is our resignation from the constituent process that is the primary cause of social injustice.*

Now, it is necessary to understand what it is, a constitution, what it is for, all citizens should know that: we, "the people", need representatives, above us, having a power to produce and apply a written law, which pacifies our society, by preventing the arbitrary domination of the strongest.

But since always, we know that these powers are not only *useful*, they are also extremely *dangerous*: all powers have a tendency to abuse, always (Montesquieu), it is like a physical law, implacable, and the great tool to protect us from the abuses of powers, it is the constitution.

The constitution is therefore a text that serves to *weaken* the powers. The constitution, in order to do its job of protection, must *worry* the powers. So they must fear it.

But then, if the powers that be should fear the constitution, they should obviously not write it! It is however easy to understand and to foresee, that political professionals, at the moment of writing themselves the rules supposed to frighten them later, these people are in CONFLICT OF INTEREST, they are at the same time *judge and parties*: in this precise case, they cannot be fair: they will obviously program their power and our impotence. And we can't even blame them: no one is strong enough to commit political hara-kiri, it's normal, anyone would do the same thing. So it is up to us, and us alone, to forbid them to write, because they will not give it up themselves! They won't. The solution will not come from them but from us.

Here it is, the cause of causes (on which we should meet to become strong): *it is not up to the men in power to write the rules of power*, we have to stop resigning on that.

So, the first decisive battle is to put all the important words "right side up":

Today, first of all, I am not a "citizen" (a citizen is *autonomous*, he votes himself his laws), I am only an "elector", that is to say a political child, I am *heteronomous*: I undergo the law voted by another than me.

My "parents" in politics, the elected officials, do not want me to emancipate myself from them, they do not want me to grow up and become autonomous: they refuse that I myself vote for or against the laws to which I submit.

I recall the coup d'état of February 4, 2008, when our so-called "representatives" imposed on us by parliamentary means the unconstitutional treaty that we had just expressly rejected by referendum in 2005. This political rape is extremely serious. And yet we have no means of resisting even this high treason.

They say we are "incompetent". They treat us like children. But it is our fault: we are perhaps, in a way, children (children believe in Santa Claus and voters believe in "universal suffrage"): we accept to call "democracy" (*demos cratos*, the power to the people) its strict opposite: the so-called modern "democracy", what is it? Well, it is the only right of :
- designate masters,
- among people we didn't choose,
- and without any means to resist a betrayal between two elections…
- with, in addition, the right of expression, it is true, but without any binding force,
- and then that's it.

The real name of this undemocratic regime is "representative government" (well, supposedly representative).

In fact, we agree to call a text that is not a constitution a constitution. We have to know what we want: the simple word constitution or the real protection it should program?

So, in order to resist properly, we have to start with what I call *the strike of lying words,* like "democracy", "universal suffrage", "citizen" and "constitution", which have been turned upside down by the thieves of power.

Our undemocratic regime is a deliberate, voluntary project, from the beginning: Sieyès (one of the most influential thinkers of the French Revolution), said in 1789: "The citizens who appoint themselves representatives renounce and must renounce making the law themselves; they have no particular will to impose. If they dictated wills, France would no longer be this representative State; it would be a democratic State. The people,

I repeat, in a country that is not a democracy (and France could not be one), the people can only speak, can only act through their representatives." (Speech of September 7, 1789).

Well, I think that's clear, don't you?

And this other quote, even more explicit, from Voltaire: "A well-organized society is one in which the few make the many work, are fed by them, and govern them." Voltaire a democrat? It's a joke, no doubt. History demonstrates in detail the imposture and the permanent tricks of the "representative government" since two hundred years: I recommend you the videos of Henri Guillemin on the Net. And these people knew very well what they were doing, they knew very well that they needed an election and not the drawing of lots: all the thinkers of the world before 1789, from Plato-Aristotle to Montesquieu-Rousseau, knew and wrote that the election is by nature aristocratic, and therefore oligarchic, and that the only procedure that is democratic is the drawing of lots, with a thousand controls on the people who are designated by lot. Read these two quotes, two thousand years apart:

Aristotle: "Elections are aristocratic, not democratic: they introduce an element of deliberate choice, of selection of the best citizens, the *aristoi*, instead of government by the whole people."

Montesquieu: "Suffrage by lot is of the nature of democracy; suffrage by choice is of that of aristocracy."

So it's not a fad of Father Chouard's... It's a question of definitions, to be respected so that words have a meaning, so that they remain "in the right place". And it's like that everywhere in the world.

To reinforce this (theoretical) idea, I would like to refer to history and to (practical) facts. We have two historical experiences, quite long, which are two laboratories: on the one hand, democracy and therefore the drawing of lots, Athens for two hundred years, two thousand five hundred years ago, and on the other hand, representative government and therefore election, also for two hundred years, since 1789. Let's look at the results:

- For two hundred years, the drawing of lots has always given power to the poorest citizens, "the 99%" (look at the two centuries of democracy in Athens, there are no exceptions).
- Whereas, for two hundred years, the election has always given power to the wealthiest citizens, "the 1%" (look at the two centuries of representative government around the world, there are no exceptions).

My central question is: *how much longer will the poor (the 99%) prefer election to lottery (against their most obvious interests)?*

Our preference for elections is literally incomprehensible. Only myths can explain it: the drawing of lots has not been taught for two hundred years in the so-called "republican" school (which preaches to us every day "elections=democracy, democracy=elections... repeat my little one..."), which explains our intellectual difficulty in integrating this unknown procedure which we all need (everywhere on earth) to get out of trouble. It takes time to detoxify.

Does the drawing of lots frighten you? To reassure you, I must warn you against a frequent misunderstanding: in a democracy, it is not the chosen ones who decide! The drawing of lots serves precisely to *weaken* the representatives (basically, those drawn by lot are those who *prepare* the laws and those who *apply* them: the civil servants, the policemen, the judges...). So, with the drawing of lots, we weaken these representatives so that they remain our servants, and that they never become our Masters. The drawing of lots guarantees that the people will remain the sovereign.

Don't be too quick to dismiss the drawing of lots in politics: there are many experiences on earth that work very well: I am thinking, for example, of British Columbia (near Vancouver), which had its entire (complex and important) electoral code rewritten in 2004 by an assembly drawn by lot: these simple citizens, frightened at the beginning, but reassured afterwards, became competent through their work, finally had tears in their eyes when they handed in their text, proud as anything to have succeeded, and obtained 57% in the referendum... All the experiences of citizens' juries drawn by lot show an indisputable competence of ordinary citizens.

But beware: to defend this idea of drawing lots (of the Constituent Assembly at least, and of the representatives afterwards, eventually), we can only count on ourselves, the normal people, at the base, those who do not want power. And here I would like to share with you this wonderful thought of Alain (the great philosopher), who said: "The most visible trait in the just man is that he does not want to govern others at all, and governs only himself. This decides everything. It might as well be said that the worst will govern. In a regime of election, which gives power to those who want it, Alain is right: the worst will rule. But on the contrary, the drawing of lots can get us out of this trap by offering power to all those who do not want it (and who are often the best among us).

We must therefore pass the word among ourselves, among "normal" people, and we must all become "trainers of trainers", in order to quickly become billions of "white blood cells" (or "nice, democratic viruses") carrying a simple and strong idea, an idea that aims precisely, with all our strength, at the Achilles' heel of the oligarchy: **we demand honesty in the constituent process, replacing election with the drawing of lots for the constituent assembly; we want to institute our political power ourselves.**

I invite you to join us on the Net: we are in the process of demonstrating that we need, and that we are capable, we want, to write our own constitution, our social contract. We'll have to continue to work on this idea, to go and find the rest on the Net and in books, to work on it... If there are really many of us, we'll just have to want it to happen, without violence.

This idea that I am building with you, it would work for all the countries of the world.

2.
The citizen trial of the election
and a defense of the drawing of lots

I would now like to describe the central - and profoundly undemocratic - procedure of representative government: the election of masters from among candidates who can be helped.

Capitalism and its appalling injustices are the economic consequence of political dispossession. Capitalism is above all law: the law of the rich, imposed by the rich, for two hundred years. What allows the rich to write the laws is a procedure, the election, which gives certain access to power to those who have the means to help the candidates. Everything else flows from that. It seems to me therefore futile to fight against the political or banking turpitudes of our representatives, when these turpitudes are only the consequences of our political dispossession.

In the Ancien Régime, the great merchants, and in particular the silver merchants, were certainly influential, but not all-powerful: they had to respect the absolute monarchy and the clergy. Economic power and political power were not in the same hands.

On the occasion of the two revolutions (American in 1776 and French in 1789), the great merchants freed themselves from their chains by writing the constitutions themselves (a fundamentally liberating gesture for all those who dared to venture freely), which allowed them to impose a procedure for the designation of representatives that was fundamentally antidemocratic and plutocratic (giving power to the rich): "election-from-among-candidates-who-can-help", candidates chosen by the richest. Capitalism is the regime in which merchants have managed to write constitutions, and therefore laws. It seems to me that this coup de force (constitutive and then legislative) is decisive, central and founding.

This plutocratic procedure of the election remains today clearly the load-bearing wall of capitalism. If the people considered themselves legitimate and capable of taking back from the rich the constituent power - and thus the legislative power - it would mechanically be the end of capitalism, simply because the great merchants and usurers would no longer be able to impose their representatives, their laws and their money on the whole society.

It is indeed the procedure of "election-from-candidates-we-can-help", which we are invited to adore like a sacred cow (electing masters instead of voting for laws), that organizes our political impotence and locks in capitalism.

According to Paul Ricoeur, "a society is democratic when it recognizes that it is divided, that is to say, when it is traversed by contradictions of interest, and when it sets itself the task of associating each citizen equally in the expression of these contradictions, in the analysis of these contradictions and in the deliberation of these contradictions, with a view to arriving at an arbitration. The definition of the common good is therefore, by construction, relative, variable, debatable, conflictual, and therefore political; it fundamentally raises the question of sovereignty: who is legitimate to make common decisions? who evaluates the needs of the social body? who decides? who evaluates the decisions? The people themselves or their representatives? Do we really need representatives?

If the size of our societies indeed requires the appointment of representatives, what kind of representatives should we choose? For the word representative is polysemous in French: should we prefer masters or servants to serve the common good? And above all, who is legitimate to decide on all these superior rules, these meta-rules of the constitution?

In theory, for the past two hundred years, advocates of "election-from-candidates" for legislators and rulers, a procedure called "universal suffrage," have claimed to serve the common good by appointing the best and controlling them, while freeing up time for the governed.

But in practice, for two hundred years, the election has produced a system of domination of the many by the few. This type of society was desired from the beginning, as early as the 18th century, by people like Voltaire (a wealthy arms dealer and an important inspiration of the French Revolution in 1789): "The spirit of a nation always resides in the few, who make the many work, are nourished by them, and govern them. Certainly this spirit of the Chinese nation is the oldest monument of reason that exists on earth[1]. Abbé Sieyès, perhaps the principal founding father of representative government, made the program of the Revolution unabashedly clear as early as 1789: "In democracy, the citizens themselves make the laws, and directly appoint the public officers. In our plan [representative government], the citizens make, more or less immediately, the choice of their deputies to the Legislative Assembly; legislation thus ceases to be democratic and becomes representative[2].

---

1. Voltaire, *Essai sur les mœurs et l'esprit des nations*, volumes 11 to 13 of *Œuvres complètes*, Paris, Éditions Garnier, 1878, *loc. cit.* t. XII, chapter CLV.
2. Abbé Sieyès, *Quelques idées de constitution applicables à la ville de Paris*, juillet 1789, à Versailles, chez Baudouin, imprimeur de l'Assemblée nationale, p. 3. https://gallica.bnf.fr/ark:/12148/bpt6k6540436h.texteImage

There are a thousand proofs of the founding fathers' desire to keep the people out of politics through election. I refer to the quotes from historical figures (chapter 7).

The best way for modern voters like us to understand the value of drawing lots in politics is to conduct the (fair) trial of the election ourselves, because this indictment, by mirror effect, shows one by one the intrinsic qualities of drawing lots[3].

We will see that the election paralyzes the governed (chapter 3) and that it gives power to the worst governors (chapter 4)... Brilliant result...

---

3. The *competition* procedure, a Chinese tradition, will not be studied here. Read Bernard Manin, *Principes du gouvernement représentatif,* Paris, Calmann-Lévy, "Liberté de l'esprit", 1995, p. 177: "It might be noted that the attribution of political authority by competition was long practiced in ancient China. The competition constitutes, beside the drawing of lots, the election, the heredity and the designation by the rulers in place, one of the possible modalities of the selection of the rulers. [...]"

3.
On the side of the governed, the election infantilizes the citizens and discourages them from thinking and defending the common good (contrary to the drawing of lots)

The election is aristocratic, while the drawing of lots is democratic

The greatest thinkers have long known what we have forgotten today.

Aristotle (332 B.C.): "Elections are aristocratic and undemocratic: they introduce an element of deliberate choice, of selection of the best citizens, the *aristoi*, instead of government by the whole people[4]."

Montesquieu (1748): "Suffrage by lot is in the nature of democracy; suffrage by choice is in the nature of aristocracy[5].

4. Aristotle, *Politics*, book IV.
5. Montesquieu, *De l'esprit des lois* (1748).

Cornelius Castoriadis (1996): "It was the Greeks who invented elections. This is a historically attested fact. They may have been wrong, but they invented elections! Who was elected in Athens? Magistrates were not elected. Magistrates were chosen by lot or by rotation. For Aristotle, remember, a citizen is one who is capable of governing and being governed. Everyone is capable of governing, so we draw lots. Why? Because politics is not a matter for specialists. There is no science of politics. There is an opinion, the doxa of the Greeks[6] "

So, the word *aristoi* means "the best" in Greek. The election which, by definition, leads to the choice of the best is thus by construction aristocratic. The promise of democratic equality is therefore not kept, elected representatives and represented are not on an equal footing: the elected dominate the electors, a few command the many; we can therefore fear that the common good is threatened, if ever the elected serve personal interests instead of serving the general interest.

On the contrary, the drawing of lots appoints anyone; it is therefore the only procedure that respects the political equality between citizens (the founding promise of democracy).

To elect is to abdicate, it is to renounce to exercise one's sovereignty, it is to delegate, it is to renounce to legislate, whereas to draw lots is to claim one's sovereignty

The word "representative" is polysemous, it can designate two very opposite powers: in French, a representative can be a servant (like a broker, an agent who faithfully waits for the orders of his principal to act), but a representative can also be a master (like a tutor, who decides everything in place of the incapable

---

6. Cornelius Castoriadis, *Post-scriptum sur l'insignifiance, Entretiens avec Daniel Mermet*, La Tour-d'Aigues, Éditions de l'Aube, 1998.

person he represents). This polysemy is the source of the most serious misunderstandings (not to say the worst political scams).

By construction, today, the "election-by-candidates" procedure produces representatives who will be masters, voting all laws in place of the voters. Whereas the drawing of lots would produce representatives who would be equals, leaving the right to pass laws to the citizens themselves. Elected representatives decide everything in place of the voters - election dispossesses the voters of their sovereignty -, whereas those drawn by lot decide only what the citizens cannot (or do not want to) decide (preparation of laws, execution of laws, individual judgments...), in other words, drawing by lot does not dispossess the citizens of their sovereignty.

Robespierre, an authentic democrat, expressed it strongly in this way: "Democracy is a state where the sovereign people, guided by laws that are their work, do by themselves all that they can do well, and by delegates all that they cannot do themselves[7].

In our "republics", voters are wrongly called "citizens", whereas a voter is heteronomous: he undergoes the law written by another; on the contrary, a citizen is autonomous: he produces himself the law he agrees to obey. Thus, the "election among candidates" reduces the people to the degrading rank of voters, a kind of political children (etymologically, child means "deprived of speech"), politically impotent: the election acts as a gag, it infantilizes us, politically, and thus also globally (socially and economically), and the election thus prevents the majority from defending in person the common good. We are not citizens, we are voters.

---

7. Maximilien Robespierre, *Sur les principes de morale politique qui doivent guider la Convention nationale dans l'administration intérieure de la République*, Convention nationale, discours du 17 pluviôse an II (5 février 1794), in *Œuvres de Maximilien Robespierre*, Publication de la Société des études robespierristes, Ivry, Phénix Éditions, 2000, tome X, p. 353.

Moreover, the founding fathers of our regime knew very well that they were going to keep the people out of the production of norms, thanks to this enslaving meaning of the word representatives. The Abbé Sieyès, an assertive antidemocrat, expressed it clearly in these terms: "Citizens who appoint themselves representatives renounce and must renounce making the law themselves; they have no particular will to impose. If they dictated wills, France would no longer be this representative State; it would be a democratic State. The people, I repeat, in a country that is not a democracy (and France could not be one), the people can only speak, can only act through their representatives[8].

Is it serious to pretend that the common good is correctly respected by keeping the majority of the population permanently and knowingly out of political reflections and decisions? Yet, there are many great thinkers who have clearly seen that decisions are better taken by a popular assembly than by a single man.

One thinks first of Aristotle: "Deliberation will indeed be better if all deliberate in common, the people with the notables, these with the masses[9].

One would also like to quote Machiavelli: "I say that a people is wiser, more constant and more wise than a prince[10].

---

8. Emmanuel-Joseph Sieyès, *Dire de l'abbé Sieyès, sur la question du veto royal,* Assemblée nationale, discours du 7 septembre 1789.
9. Aristotle, *Politics*, book IV, 14, 1298-b.
10. Machiavelli, *Discourse on the First Decade of Titus Livius* (1531), book I, chap. LVIII: "The crowd is wiser and more constant than a prince".

The election infantilizes, discourages and disempowers, discourages to do well, distances the people from politics and the common good, while the drawing of lots encourages, empowers and incites to do well

The election is a pedagogy of servitude, a learning of resignation, it locks the voters in a role of dominated. By infantilizing them, the election *disempowers* the voters.

On the contrary, the drawing of lots emancipates citizens, treating them as responsible adults. And in general, people try to be worthy of the trust placed in them, especially if they are entrusted with real responsibility. The experiences of the citizens' conventions organized by Jacques Testart show that the level rises quickly when people are really respected and involved.

Jacques Testart: "What is extraordinary when we are interested in citizens' conferences (drawn by lot and charged with giving an opinion on the political and social stakes of a scientific subject), is to see to what extent individuals can be modified during the procedure. You take a baker, a teacher, well people who have their job and who *a priori* are innocent, naive with regard to the problem. It is not so much that they become competent, that is obvious. It is mainly that they become another quality of human. That is to say, they develop ideas and points of view, they defend their opinion, they are not at all there to defend their family, not even their children, but the descendants of everyone else... We see a kind of altruism that shines through, that we don't usually see.

And what I noticed while looking at this is how much of a mess humanity is. That is to say, we keep people in a state of stupidity, of following, of conditioning. And I have to say, I didn't believe it until I saw it. I thought it was sad but that humanity was not beautiful to see. But it's not beautiful to see because we put it in that state. I am now convinced that there is something in most people that we don't tap into, that we don't use, that we don't bring out. But humans are worth much more than what we make of them[11].

Tocqueville, too, wrote admirable pages defending the educational and empowering virtues of civil juries drawn by lot. "By jury, I mean a certain number of citizens taken at random and temporarily invested with the right to judge. [The jury, and especially the civil jury, serves to give to the minds of all citizens a part of the habits of the mind of the judge; and these habits are precisely those which best prepare the people to be free. It spreads in all classes respect for the judged thing and the idea of right. Take away these two things, and the love of independence will be nothing but a destructive passion. It teaches men the practice of equity. Everyone, in judging his neighbor, thinks that he can be judged in turn. [...] The jury teaches each man not to shrink from the responsibility of his own actions; a virile disposition, without which there is no political virtue. [...] By forcing men to concern themselves with something other than their own affairs, it combats individual egoism, which is like the rust of societies. The jury serves incredibly well to train the judgment and increase the natural enlightenment of the people. This, in my opinion, is its greatest advantage. It must be considered as a free and always open school, where each juror comes to learn about his rights, where he comes into daily communication with the most educated and enlightened members of the higher classes, where the laws are taught to him in a practical way [...] Thus the jury, which is the most energetic means of making the people reign, is also the most effective means of teaching them to reign[12]."

---

11. Jacques Testart, in the program *À voix nue*, France Culture, June 8, 2012.
12. Alexis de Tocqueville, *De la démocratie en Amérique*, tome 1, second part, chapter VIII, Paris, Gallimard, "Folio histoire", 2000, *loc. cit.* , p. 404-410.

Thus, on the side of the governed, by each of these first three characteristics of the election-by-candidates (aristocratic, infantilizing and demotivating procedure), we see that the election reduces to almost nothing the number of persons capable of defending the common good.

4.
On the side of the rulers, the election brings to power the worst (contrary to the drawing of lots)

On the side of the rulers, admitting that we need "representatives", we often notice that the election among candidates brings to power the worst, the exact opposite of what it claims. I see seven characteristics of elections that lead to this disaster (and I see, as if in a mirror, seven opposite characteristics of drawing lots that would avoid this disaster):

Election gives power to those who want it (drawing lots does not)

It has been known for two and a half thousand years that power should not be given to those who want it.

Plato: "The worst evil is that power is held by those who wanted it[13].

Alain: "The most visible trait in the just man is that he does not want to govern others at all and governs only himself.

---

13. Plato, quoted by Jacques Rancière, in *Siné Hebdo*, 11 March 2009.

This decides everything. You might as well say that the worst will govern[14].

The worst will rule, but only if we give power to those who want it (because the best do not). Precisely, the drawing of lots avoids this central trap and gives the power "to the others"... The drawing of lots does not condemn us to the tyranny of those who want to decide everything in the place of the others.

It is a bad idea to give power to those who want it badly enough to achieve it because the skills (and motivations) needed to achieve power (to win an electoral contest) are surely not the same as those needed to exercise power (to seek and serve the common good).

Elections encourage lying and favor liars (the lottery does not)

By relying on the will of the citizens to designate the actors, the election gives a foothold to swindlers, whose talent is precisely to know how to deceive the will. In a certain way, the election offers power to liars: it is the one who will lie the best who will be elected, every time. So, by construction, the election encourages lying: first lies *before* the mandate to be elected, and then lies *during* and *after* the mandate to be re-elected. Scientifically, mechanically, the "election-among-candidates" encourages lying, all the time.

On the other hand, by not relying on the will of the people, the drawing of lots removes any hold on the crooks. Better still, the drawing of lots dissuades people from lying, since lying is of no use in gaining access to power. It will be objected that there will always be liars in a human society. Of course, but the

---

14. Alain, *Propos sur les pouvoirs. Éléments d'éthique politique* (1925), Paris, Gallimard, "Folio essais", 1985.

drawing of lots reduces the proportion of liars in power, which can only be beneficial to the common good.

Election produces masters (whereas drawing lots produces equals)

Having been designated as the best, the chosen one naturally, and quite logically, experiences pride, vanity and a feeling of superiority, moods which naturally incite him to feel legitimate to decide everything, all alone, without having to demonstrate further that he is worthy of his office. Many abuses of power - and many neglects of the common good - are undoubtedly deeply rooted in this feeling of superiority of the "chosen one", which is necessarily born of this aristocratic procedure that is election among candidates.

On the contrary, the drawing of lots offers no reason to feel superior and therefore encourages the representative to be humble: one has not been chosen as the best, but as an equal, and one must therefore demonstrate at all times that one is worthy of the office.

For two hundred years, we have noticed that elections produce assemblies of notables, absolutely not representative of the social body they claim to represent, and what is more, extremely privileged. There are countless scientific studies that prove the glaring absence of the working classes in Parliament, as well as journalistic investigations that prove the countless (and shameful) advantages that parliamentarians grant themselves.

One of the meanings of the word represent is to reconstruct a faithful miniature image of the society represented. The drawing of lots is for this purpose much better adapted than the election. It alone is capable of composing a representative sample of the whole of the citizens. Drawing lots for an assembly will always give 50% women, 90% employees and 10% unemployed.

The question of whether the assembly that will represent us should look like us or not is a sovereign choice of the constituent citizens and not of the elected officials.

The election produces uncontrolled teachers
(not the drawing of lots)

Election is based on trust and places control over representatives precisely at the time of their appointment. This choice discourages further control of elected officials, both during and after their term of office: one hears that election and the risk of non-re-election are quite sufficient controls... This absence of real controls on elected officials makes corruption possible - and even encourages it. Election without controls other than election does not properly protect the common good.

Whereas the drawing of lots, naturally inspiring mistrust, shifts the moment of the control of the representatives: the control of those drawn by lot does not take place at the moment of the designation (anyone is chosen), but at any moment, during the mandate and after the mandate (by other drawn). It thus appears that those drawn by lot are naturally and instinctively much more controlled than those elected.

This essential difference (concerning controls) logically leads to the recommendation of election among candidates to designate local representatives (whom one knows, knows and can observe more easily oneself because of the proximity), and to the recommendation of drawing lots (and its multiple controls at all levels) to designate representatives at the regional, national or federal level (whom one does not know and cannot supervise oneself because of the distance).

Thus, election is well suited to municipal elections (and poorly suited to others), while lottery is much better suited to regional, national and federal elections. We usually hear the opposite, and it is wrong.

The election produces a caste of masters out of control (not the drawing of lots)

In all the polls, in all our conversations, the most frequent and most serious reproach that citizens make to representative government is the professionalization of politics. But this professionalization is an inescapable consequence of the election. The same reasons that led to the election of a candidate once (the short list of willing candidates, their art of seduction, which is constantly being perfected, the personality of the voters, who hardly change from one election to the next) lead to the re-election of a candidate several times. The election thus counteracts the rotation of offices, which mechanically imposes the professionalization of politics - and the formation of parties, to which we will return in a moment. This has been observed throughout the world and in all periods.

The election denies political equality by depriving the greatest number of people of political action for the benefit of a political caste.

The drawing of lots imposes the rotation of offices and thus prohibits the professionalization of politics. It respects the political equality of citizens by prohibiting any formation of privileged caste.

The election imposes parties to win the political war, with a military logic claiming the obedience of the militants and mobilizing the collective passions (not the drawing of lots)

We vote almost once a year; and a single citizen cannot win an "election among candidates". As a result, the permanent electoral campaign that follows from the choice of the election (as a procedure for the designation of representatives) imposes on the candidates to mobilize an army of militants, enlisted around a leader, a line of thought, a dogma, a discipline, a hierarchy, the detestation of all other equivalent armies (en bloc), the sectarian obsession to reach power alone, etc., which maintains the discord. The common good is no longer followed when the priority objective is to achieve power.

Parties are only for winning elections and nothing else. There have never been parties in systems without elections. It is the choice of election that condemns us to the plague of parties, but we obviously do not need parties to make politics... That is why, with the drawing of lots, parties become useless and disappear naturally.

The election allows to help a candidate, and thus gives the power to the richest (not the drawing of lots)

It is easy to bribe someone who owes you everything. It is difficult to bribe someone who owes you nothing. If one can help a candidate, it is certain that those who have the means to help will always do so, because the elected officials "helped" will thus necessarily be debtors - and therefore servants - of the private interests of their benefactors (whom they absolutely need, for their election and for their re-election).

What are some ways to help certain candidates? It is a matter of showing them a lot, of showing them in a flattering light (of asking them only easy questions, without traps), of discrediting or not inviting their competitors, etc. All this "work" of opinion[15] is done by the big media (press, radio, television, polling institutes) and their "journalists" "editorialists" and other "experts". Today, all the press and publishing belong to a few banks and industrialists and to two arms dealers[16].

---

15. Serge Halimi, Henri Maler, Mathias Reymond, Dominique Vidal, *L'opinion, ça se travaille... Les médias et les " guerres justes "*, Marseille, Agone 2014. See also, Noam Chomsky and Edward Herman, *De la propagande médiatique en démocratie*, Marseille, Agone, 2008.
16. Geoffrey Geuens, *Tous pouvoirs confondus. État, capital et médias à l'ère de la mondialisation*, Brussels, EPO Editions, 2003.

Thus, the election among candidates allows, and even incites, corruption. This is probably its most serious and unforgivable flaw. The richest individuals of the social body have thus found in "election-from-candidates" the sure means to keep power forever, and to produce a right that is favorable to them. One can call this right "capitalism" or plutocracy (government by the rich for the rich), but the whole pyramid of instituted powers (parliament, government, judges, prisons, police…) is due to the procedure of designation of the legislators: nothing imposes on the 99% of the population to prefer the election rather than the drawing of lots; it is elected officials who have chosen the election procedure… One can easily understand them, moreover, because of their personal interest, but this choice has nothing to do with the common good and we are not obliged to follow them in this choice.

On the other hand, the drawing of lots, which does not allow anyone to be helped, is an egalitarian and incorruptible procedure which brings to power better servants of the common good, less corruptible because they owe nothing to anyone for their accession to power.

The "election-by-candidates" brings to power people who will defend particular interests, while the drawing of lots brings to power people who will defend the general interest.

Of course, nothing is perfect and the risks of corruption will always exist, in any human society, but it is clear that the "election among candidates" accumulates all the vices, from the point of view of the common good (not from the point of view of the elected representatives, of course, nor of their rich benefactors). It is reasonable to expect that the drawing of lots will reduce the ratio of corrupt people in power.

Conclusion

We have two political laboratories to verify in the field that practice confirms what theory predicts: *200 years of* (daily) *drawing of lots* in Athens (in the 5th and 4th centuries B.C.) allowed poor citizens (today, we would say the 99%) to govern for the whole period; while, on the contrary, *200 years of "elections among candidates"* (since 1789) allowed rich citizens (today, we would say the 1%) to govern for the whole period. Thus, in theory and in practice, elections give power to the rich (the 1%), and the drawing of lots gives power to the poor (the 99%).

Aristotle writes: "Reasoning thus makes it evident, it seems, that the sovereignty of a minority or a majority is only an accident, peculiar either to oligarchies or to democracies, due to the fact that everywhere the rich are in the minority and the poor in the majority. Therefore, the real difference between democracy and oligarchy is poverty and wealth; and necessarily, a regime in which the rulers, whether they are a majority or a minority, exercise power through their wealth is an oligarchy, and one in which the poor rule a democracy[17]."

An important question then comes to mind: "How much longer will the 99% defend as a democratic sacred cow the aristocratic procedure that infantilizes them forever and paralyzes them forever?"

---

17. Aristotle, *Politics*, Book III, quoted by Moses I. Finley, *Democracy Ancient and Modern*, Brunswick, New Jersey, Rutgers University Press, 1973; translated into French as *Démocratie antique et démocratie moderne* (1976), Paris, Payot, "Petite bibliothèque Payot", 2003.

5.
The different practices
of the draw

It remains to examine the different practices of drawing lots in politics. After the surprise, for the common good, to see itself so badly served by election, and so well defended by the drawing of lots, one can ask oneself what are the main uses of a random procedure of designation of representatives, and how this procedure could be one day really instituted, written in the constitution.

"Election-from-candidates" usually assigns privileges, while the lottery most often distributes offices.

It is important to keep in mind that, to hold a position or fulfill a function, one always elects a single person (whom one trusts and controls little or not at all) for a fairly long time; whereas one often draws lots for a collective of people (whom one distrusts and controls really and often) for a fairly short time - which reassures everyone... We will point out here three main cases, keeping the most important, the most decisive, for the end.

Drawing of lots to designate
the Chambers of Control of all powers

There is no lack of references in the literature of political philosophy to insist on the great duty of vigilance of citizens against all powers. We can quote:

Montesquieu: "It is an eternal experience that every man who has power is inclined to abuse it; he goes so far as to find limits. Who would say so! Virtue itself needs limits. For power not to be abused, it is necessary that, by the disposition of things, power stops power[18].

Alain: "Any leader will be a detestable tyrant if he is allowed to do so[19].

Machiavelli: "The best fortress of tyrants is the inertia of the people. Whoever wants to found a state and give it laws must assume in advance that men are wicked and always ready to display this character of wickedness."

Marat: "Watching is the first duty of every good citizen."

Madame Roland in 1789: "Representative government soon becomes the most corrupt of governments if the people cease to inspect their representatives. The problem with the French is that they give too much to trust, and that is how freedom is lost. It is true that this trust is infinitely convenient: it dispenses with the care of watching, thinking and judging."

Gandhi: "True democracy will come not from the empowerment of a few but from the power of all to oppose the abuse of power."

Robespierre: "What do we care about the combinations that balance the authority of tyrants? It is tyranny that must be extirpated. It is not in the quarrel of their masters that the people must seek the advantage of breathing for a few moments,

---

18. Montesquieu, *De l'esprit des lois*, book XI, chap. IV.
19. Alain, *Propos sur les pouvoirs, op. cit.*

it is in their own forces that the guarantee of their rights must be placed. [...] There is only one tribune of the people that I can confess; it is the people themselves[20] [...]" or again: "The source of all our evils, it is the absolute independence in which the representatives have put themselves with regard to the nation without having consulted it. They have recognized the sovereignty of the nation, and they have annihilated it. They were, by their own admission, only representatives of the people, and they have made themselves sovereign, that is to say despots, because despotism is nothing other than the usurpation of sovereign power[21] [...] ".

Rousseau: "As soon as public service ceases to be the main concern of citizens, and they prefer to serve with their purse rather than with their person, the State is already close to ruin. Should we go to war? They pay troops and stay at home; should we go to the Council? They appoint deputies and stay at home. By dint of laziness and money, they finally have soldiers to enslave the country, and representatives to sell it[22]."

Because of conflict of interest and esprit de corps, a power will never (can never) be properly judged by its peers.

The universal antidote to conflicts of interest is the drawing of lots; this is why everyone (except the powers that be, of course) quickly understands and admits the interest and importance of this first use of chance in politics: in the perspective of the common good, it is necessary that all the control organs of

---

20. Maximilien Robespierre, *Sur la Constitution*, Convention nationale, speech of May 10, 1793, in *Œuvres de Maximilien Robespierre, op. cit.* volume IX, p. 499 and p. 500.

21. Maximilien Robespierre, *Sur la déchéance du roi et le renouvellement de la législature - Des maux et des ressources de l'État*, Société des Amis de la Constitution, speech of July 29, 1792, in *Œuvres de Maximilien Robespierre, op. cit.* volume VIII, p. 416.

22. Jean-Jacques Rousseau, *Du contrat social* (1762), Paris, Éditions Garnier Frères, 1962, book III, chap. XV, p. 301.

the various powers be composed of ordinary citizens, and thus drawn by lot (and trained for that).

Drawing of lots to designate all or part of the Legislative Body

The point of drawing lots for the legislature is a delicate one, and therefore controversial: we have so long believed, despite all evidence to the contrary, that electing legislators ourselves was a good way to serve the common good, that we now find it hard to imagine that a Parliament drawn by lot would give the public interest a better chance than an elected Parliament. Besides, there are plenty of people who don't want to do the job...

Thus, this particular use of the lottery is the most time-consuming (and sometimes impossible) to accept, and often it is only accepted by people who discover it through the compromise of two legislative chambers: one elected (the House of Parties) and one drawn by lot (the House of Citizens). It is an open field, with many opportunities for intelligent innovation.

If this use of lottery frightens you or puts you off, do not reject all uses of lottery: you have the right to qualify your thinking, and you may want one use of lottery (for the Houses of Control and for the Constituent Assembly, for example) while rejecting another (for the Legislative Chamber, for example).

Drawing of lots to designate the Constituent Assembly, without which nothing will happen

The most important use of the drawing of lots in politics is undoubtedly that of the appointment of the Constituent Assembly. It is the most important one because it is the very condition for all other uses of the drawing of lots to happen (elected officials will never give up the procedure that gives them power).

We recall that the constitution is the superior text that institutes all the powers of a country, that fixes the procedures for designating the actors, the organs for controlling these actors, and the power of the people in relation to these powers. The constitution is a social contract, always subject to revision, by which a human group constitutes itself by establishing the powers it agrees to obey. The constitution must imperatively limit the powers, to protect society against their abuse: therefore, it must never be the men in power who write the rules of power (the constitution): indeed, in the constitutive process, the elected officials are necessarily in conflict of interests (they have a personal interest contrary to the general interest), and they will always institute their power and the popular powerlessness. This is precisely what we observe, all over the world and at all times.

There is almost no trace of this radical idea in the literature, but I have found one that I would like to point out. It was Thomas Paine, an Englishman, who wrote in 1791: "It is contrary to the principles of representative government for a body to grant powers to itself[23]. And: "A government has no right to take part in a debate as to the principles or method of making or amending a constitution. It is not for the benefit of those who exercise governmental power that constitutions and the governments that flow from them are made. In all these things, the right to judge and act belongs to those who pay and not to those who receive[24]. And again: "There is no other contract than the one made between its different components by the people as a whole in order to generate and constitute a government. To suppose that any government can be a party to a contract with the people is to suppose that the government existed before it had the right to do so. Government is not a business which any man or group of men have the right to open and manage for

____

23. Thomas Paine, *The Rights of Man* (1791-1792), Paris, Belin, "Alpha", 2009.
24. *Id. in ibid.* chapter 4: "Of the constitutions", p. 267 ff.

their own benefit. It is but a deposit, entrusted in the name of those who delegate it - and who at any time may take it back[25]."

Today, I say it this way: it is *not up to the men in power to write the rules of power*. If the drawing of lots has never been instituted, it is undoubtedly because Constituent Assemblies have always been elected from among professional political candidates, whose self-interest leads them to naturally prefer the election, at the expense of the common good.

So, if the peoples of the world want to get out of the political trap that condemns them to impotence, they will undoubtedly have to make the drawing of lots for the Constituent Assembly their absolute priority: in order to finally institute the right of peoples to self-determination (really), the Constituent Assemblies must not be elected from among candidates. Who will carry this project of a citizen Constituent Assembly, if not the citizens themselves?

---

25. *Ibid.*

6.
Constituent workshops
as practical tools for popular education

The regime of representative government (wrongly called "representative democracy", a misleading oxymoron), a regime of domination of the electorate by elected officials, was wanted and imposed from the beginning only by elected officials (Sieyes, Madison…). The solution will therefore not come from the elected, who are the problem as long as they confiscate the constituent power. The solution can only come from others, that is to say from the citizens themselves. The emancipation of voters (their mutation into citizens) requires that their political power be instituted, and it is therefore necessary that voters train themselves to be constituents.

A citizen worthy of the name must be vigilant, therefore constituting

Vigilance has long been recognized as an essential quality of citizenship:

Plato: "The punishment for good people who are not interested in politics is to be governed by bad people."

Thucydides: "A man who does not meddle in politics deserves to be called, not a peaceful citizen, but a useless one[26].

Marat: "To remain free, one must be constantly on guard against those who govern: nothing is easier than to lose the one who is without distrust; and the too great security of the people is always the precursor of their servitude[27].

Alain: "Democracy is not in the popular origin of power, it is in its control. Democracy is the exercise of control by the governed over the governors. Not once every five years, not every year, but every day[28].

We must all be vigilant, on a daily basis. But how effective is vigilance without the power to act? Today, our anti-constitutions do not recognize any power to the voters to defend themselves against the politicians. In order to play their role of sentinels of democracy, citizens must therefore acquire a guaranteed power (whatever the choice made about the representatives - masters or servants).

In Athens, it was the *Ecclesia*, the assembly of the people, whose role was to vote the laws but also to implement the *isègoria*, the right to speak for all, at any time and on any subject, allowing each citizen to become in case of danger a sentinel of the democracy, a guardian of the common good.

Today, this instituted popular power could take the form of freedom of expression, the citizens' initiative referendum, public media accessible to all, and the protective status of whistle-blowers, for example.

Elected officials will never institute the power of citizens. Only citizens are capable of instituting their own power. It is thus quite decisive (and non-negotiable) that the citizens are

---

26. Thucydides 2.40.2, trans. Roussel and Pierre Vidal-Naquet, *in* Moses I Finley, *Démocratie antique et démocratie moderne, op.cit.*
27. Jean-Paul Marat, *The Chains of Slavery* (1774).
28. Alain, *Propos sur les pouvoirs, op.cit.*

constituents, that is to say capable of wanting, instituting and defending themselves their social contract, their constitution, the superior text which constitutes them as a people.

This will require learning - both theoretical and practical - for the population. How can this be done?

This mutation of voters-children into citizens-adults can only happen through practical popular education: the constituent mini-workshops, prolific and contagious

Elected officials will never teach voters to do without them, nor even to control them effectively (because of the conflict of interest). It is therefore up to the citizens to train each other, among themselves, through targeted meetings on the writing of articles of constitution, "contagious" constituent mini-workshops, by popular education, among equals.

Once the multitude has been formed, accustomed to constituent debates, it will appear natural to the social body to draw by lot the citizens of the Constituent Assembly, because experience will have shown that, globally, we all write more or less the same articles. The constituent workshops thus take at the root the evil of *the popular impotence to defend the common good*. I have been running such workshops for years, all over the French-speaking world.

The common good needs many willing guardians, capable of understanding it, of wanting it and of defending it. It is therefore a political learning, theoretical and practical, autonomous, emancipating, that must not only be allowed but encouraged from the youngest age and until the end of life.

From this point of view, and at the end of this examination, *election from among candidates* reduces to almost nothing the number of these guardians of the common good and exposes them to the most serious corruptions. On the contrary, the drawing of lots, especially for the Constituent Assembly, multiplies these guardians of the general good and protects them from corruption by "disincentives" to lie and by permanent controls.

This analysis is a recent work in progress (it all started in 2005) and must not become a domain of experts: you can, and should, all participate in enriching and strengthening this reflection.

7.
Reference texts - democracy, elections, lottery *"Tell me what you read, I'll tell you who you are*

There are too many amazing texts since two thousand five hundred years on election, on the drawing of lots, on democracy, on the very necessary citizen vigilance against powers, to quote them all in an indictment like the one above (chapters 2 to 6). Here are some pearls (that you could, to tame all these ideas, play to place yourself at the right place in the indictment).

Sovereignty and democracy

"In a democracy, all the inhabitants who are sons of citizens, all those who were born on the national soil, have rendered service to the state, or for any other reason should enjoy the right of citizenship, all of them - I repeat - can rely on the law to claim the right to vote in the supreme assembly and to stand for election to the various offices" (Baruch Spinoza, *Tractatus politicus*, 1677, chap. II, § 1).

*

"It is a fundamental law of democracy that the people make the laws" (Montesquieu, *De l'esprit des lois*, 1748, book II, chap. II.)

*

"Power must be clearly distinguished from functions; the nation does indeed delegate the various public functions; but power cannot be alienated or delegated. If these powers could be delegated in detail, it would follow that sovereignty could be delegated." (Maximilien Robespierre, "Notes manuscrites en marge du projet de Constitution française de 1791," in-4°, 59 p.).

*

"Sovereignty cannot be represented, for the same reason that it can be alienated; it consists essentially in the general will, and the will cannot be represented: it is the same, or it is different; there is no middle ground. The deputies of the people are not and cannot be their representatives; they are only their commissioners; they cannot conclude anything definitively. Any law that the people themselves have not ratified is void; it is not a law. The English people think they are free, but they are very much mistaken; they are only free during the election of members of Parliament: as soon as they are elected, they are slaves, they are nothing. In the short moments of their freedom, the use they make of it is well worth losing" (Jean-Jacques Rousseau, *The Social Contract* (1762), Book III, chap. XV).

*

"I know of no other sure repository of supreme power in a society than the people themselves, and if we do not think them competent enough to exercise their control freely, the remedy is not to take it away from them, but to instruct them" (Thomas Jefferson, "Letter to William Jarvis," 1820).

*

"Democracy: a kind of government where the people have all the authority. Democracy has flourished only in the republics of Rome and Athens" (Antoine Furetière, *Dictionnaire universel*, 1690).

*

"The democrat, after all, is the one who admits that an adversary may be right, who therefore lets him express himself and who agrees to reflect on his arguments. When parties or men are convinced enough of their reasons to agree to close the mouths of their opponents by violence, then democracy is no more" (Albert Camus, excerpt from "Démocratie et Modestie", in *Combat*, February 1947).

*

"For both authors [Montesquieu and Rousseau], the concept of democracy, apprehended from the idea of sovereignty, implies that the people are themselves legislators and magistrates, that they exercise both executive and legislative power" (Pierre Rosanvallon, "Histoire du mot démocratie", *in* Pierre Rosanvallon, Pierre Manent, Marcel Gauchet, *Situations de la démocratie*, Paris, Seuil, 1993, p. 12).

*

"In States that juxtapose the legislative power of the Houses with the possibility of popular demands for referendums, it is the people who rise to supreme rank through the acquisition of the power to pronounce the rejection or definitive adoption of parliamentary decisions. As a result, Parliament is reduced to the rank of a simple authority: it no longer represents the general will except to seek and propose the expression that should be given to it; it thus fulfills the role of a civil servant. The real sovereign is then the people" (Raymond Carré de Malberg, in a 1931 article: "Référendum d'initiative populaire", quoted in Marion Paoletti, *La démocratie locale et le référendum*, Paris, L'Harmattan, "Logiques politiques", 1997, p. 89).

*

"A people is all the more democratic that deliberation, that reflection, that the critical spirit, play a more considerable role in the running of public affairs. It is all the less so when unconsciousness, unacknowledged habits, obscure feelings, prejudices, in a word, which are removed from examination, are on the contrary predominant" (Émile Durkheim, *Leçons de sociologie : physique des mœurs et du droit*, Paris, PUF, 1950, p. 123).

*

"The democratic regime can only be conceived, created and sustained by men who know that they do not know everything. The democrat is modest, he admits a certain amount of ignorance, he recognizes the partly adventurous character of his effort and that not everything is given to him, and from this admission, he recognizes that he needs to consult others, to complete what he knows" (Albert Camus, excerpt from "Reflections on a democracy without catechism", in *La Gauche*, July 1948)

*

"We have conquered universal suffrage, we still have to conquer popular sovereignty" (Jean Jaurès).

*

Through **subsidiarity**, the sovereign protects its sovereignty:

- or from above, like the pope whose social doctrine decides that a leader must not do what his subordinates can do themselves,

- or from below, like the Swiss cantons, which require that they themselves pass all the laws they can pass and that they delegate to the higher level only what they rationally have to delegate.

Instead of "Political sovereignty resides in the nation", I would propose "Legitimacy is constituted by the free consent of the people to all the authorities to which they are subject". That at least, it seems to me, means something. (Simone Weil, "Remarks on the New Draft Constitution" in *London Writings*, p 87.

Necessary vigilance of the citizens and indispensable controls of the powers in democracy

"Representative government soon becomes the most corrupt of governments if the people stop inspecting their representatives. The problem with the French is that they give too much to trust, and that is how freedom is lost. It is true that this trust is infinitely convenient: it dispenses with the care of watching, thinking and judging" (Madame Roland, 1789).

*

"Learn, therefore, that except for what concerns military discipline, that is to say, the handling and holding of arms, exercises and evolutions, the march against the enemies of the laws and of the State, the soldiers of the fatherland owe no obedience to their chiefs; that far from being subject to them, they are their arbiters; that their duty as citizens obliges them to examine the orders they receive, to weigh the consequences, to prevent the consequences. Thus, when these orders are suspicious, they must remain inactive; when these orders injure the rights of man, they must formally refuse them; when these orders endanger

59

public liberty, they must punish the authors; when these orders are detrimental to the country, they must turn their weapons against their officers. Any oath contrary to these sacred duties is a sacrilege that must render odious the one who demands it, and contemptible the one who takes it" (Jean-Paul Marat, *L'Ami du peuple*, July 8, 1790).

*

"The chances of error are even more numerous when the people delegate the exercise of legislative power to a small number of individuals; that is, when it is only by fiction that the law is the expression of the general will. [Under representative government, especially, that is, when it is not the people who make the laws, but a body of representatives, the exercise of this sacred right [the free communication of thoughts among citizens] is the only safeguard of the people against the scourge of oligarchy. Since it is in the nature of things that representatives can put their particular will in the place of the general will, it is necessary that the voice of public opinion resound constantly around them, to balance the power of personal interest and individual passions ; to remind them of the purpose of their mission and the principle of their authority" (Maximilien Robespierre, *Le Défenseur de la Constitution*, n° 5, "Sur le respect dû aux lois et aux autorités constituées" (June 1792), in *Œuvres de Maximilien Robespierre*, Publication de la Société des études robespierristes, Phénix Éditions, 2000, tome IV, p. 145-146).

*

"Whatever the names of the public officials and the external forms of government, in any State where the sovereign retains no means of repressing the abuse of his power by his delegates and of stopping their attacks against the constitution of the State, the nation is enslaved, since it is left absolutely at the mercy of those who exercise authority. And since it is in the nature of things that men prefer their personal interest to the public interest when they can do so with impunity, it follows that the people are oppressed whenever their representatives are absolutely independent of them.

If the nation has not yet reaped the fruits of the revolution, if intriguers have replaced other intriguers, if a legal tyranny seems to have succeeded the old despotism do not seek the cause elsewhere than in the privilege that the representatives of the people have arrogated to themselves to play with impunity with the rights of those whom they have basely caressed during the elections" (Maximilien Robespierre, *On the deposition of the king and the renewal of the legislature - Of the evils and the resources of the State*, Society of the Friends of the Constitution, speech of July 29, 1792)

*

"In any magistracy, the greatness of power must be compensated by the brevity of its duration. One year is the time that most legislators have fixed; a longer time would be dangerous, a shorter one would be against the nature of the thing" (Montesquieu, *De l'esprit des lois*, book II: "Des lois qui dérivent directement de la nature du gouvernement", chapter III: "Des lois relatives à la nature de l'aristocratie").

*

"The right of citizens to assemble wherever and whenever they please, in order to deal with public matters, is inherent in all free people. Without this sacred right, the State is dissolved, and the sovereign is annihilated; for, as soon as the citizens can no longer show themselves as a body, there remain in the State only isolated individuals; the nation no longer exists. One sees with what skill the conscript fathers have annihilated the sovereignty of the people, while appearing to assure individual liberty. In England, any peaceful assembly is lawful: the law forbids only seditious gatherings. That is freedom" (Jean-Paul Marat, August 16-17, 1792).

*

"All power is evil as soon as it is allowed to do so; all power is wise as soon as it feels it is being judged [...] Democracy is not in the popular origin of power, it is in its control. Democracy is the exercise of control by the governed over the governors. Not once every five years, not every year, but every day [...] Real freedom presupposes an organization constantly directed against power. Freedom dies if it does not act" (Alain, *Propos de politique*, 1934).

*

"The important thing is to build a little barricade every day, or, if you like, to bring some king before the people's court every day. Let's say that by preventing a stone from being added to the Bastille every day, we save ourselves the trouble of demolishing it" (Alain, 1925).

*

"Man does not risk falling asleep in a totalitarian world but waking up in a universe that has become totalitarian during his sleep" (Arthur Koestler).

*

"What is well known in general is, for this reason that it is well known, not known. In the process of knowledge, the most common way to deceive oneself and others is to presuppose something as known and to accept it as such." (G. F. Hegel, *Phenomenology of Spirit*).

*

"All power is wicked as soon as it is allowed to do so; all power is wise as soon as it feels itself judged." (Émile Chartier dit "Alain," *Propos*, January 25, 1930).

Anti-democratic plans of the founding fathers of representative government

"If the governed crowd can believe itself to be the equal of the few who govern, then there is no more government. Power must be beyond the comprehension of the governed crowd. Authority must be constantly kept above critical judgment through the psychological instruments of religion, patriotism, tradition, and prejudice [...] The reason of the people must not be cultivated, but their feelings, so they must be directed and their hearts not their minds must be formed." (Joseph de Maistre, "Étude sur la souveraineté", in *Œuvres complètes*, Lyon, 1891-1892, tome 1, p. 354 ff, quoted in Fabrice Arfi, *Le sens des affaires. Voyage au bout de la corruption*, Paris, Calmann-Lévy, 2014, p. 71).

*

"What will we have gained by destroying the aristocracy of the nobles, if it is replaced by the aristocracy of the rich?" (Jean-Paul Marat (1790), quoted by Jean Massin, *Jean-Paul Marat*, Livre Club Diderot, 1975, p. 28).

*

"It is the philosophy of a beggar who would like the rich to be robbed by the poor" (Voltaire, about the *Discourse on the origin of inequalities among men* by Jean-Jacques Rousseau, quoted by Henri Guillemin).

*

"It is very good to make men believe that they have an immortal soul and that there is a vengeful God who will punish my peasants if they steal my wheat and my wine" (Voltaire, quoted by Henri Guillemin, *Éclaircissements*, Paris, Gallimard, 1961).

*

"I believe that we do not agree on the article of the people, whom you believe to be worthy of instruction. By people I mean the rabble, who have only their arms to live on. I doubt that this order of citizens will ever have the time or the ability to educate themselves; they would die of hunger before becoming philosophers. It seems to me essential that there be ignorant beggars. If you were a farmer like me, and if you had ploughs, you would agree with me. It is not the labourer who must be instructed, it is the good bourgeois, it is the inhabitant of the cities; [...] When the rabble interferes with reasoning, all is lost" (Voltaire, "Letter to M. Damillaville", April 1, 1766, in *Œuvres de Voltaire*, Paris, éd. Lefèvre, 1828, tome 69, p. 131)

*

"As a theorist of state power, Carré de Malberg showed in a definitive way how the phenomenon of power - which today political science strives to define in the diversity of its raw manifestations - finds its perfect expression in the state. The State is not only the place of domination; it is also the apparatus that makes it possible to control it because, through the constitution, it imposes a status on the rulers. This status defines at the same time the finality and the modalities of their action, hence the thesis supported by Carré de Malberg concerning the self-limitation of the State. However, the constitution must be the work of the people, and the rulers must not be free to interpret it in a way that favors their will to power. It is precisely the disregard of these conditions, deliberately maintained since 1791 by French politicians, that led to the regime of the Third Republic, where Parliament substituted its own sovereignty for that of the nation. The law, expression of the general will, brings the demonstration of this intellectual swindle. He reveals its origin (a falsified definition of the general will), he describes its instrument (a partial conception of representation); he exposes its consequences (a theory of legality which has for effect to subordinate all the state authorities to the arbitrary will of the Parliament). The demonstration calls into question almost the entire constitutional order of our country and, for this reason, the work that we are about to read is not simply devoted to a specific and limited problem; it is a true treatise on French public law. A treatise which, by the wealth of its information, the rigor of its construction and the perfection of its style, constitutes an irreplaceable source of knowledge as well as a joy for the mind" (Georges Burdeau, Preface to Raymond Carré de Malberg, *La Loi, expression de la volonté générale*, 1931, reedited Paris, Economica, "Classiques", 1984).

*

"Our contemporaries are incessantly worked by two enemy passions: they feel the need to be led and the desire to remain free. Unable to destroy either of these contrary instincts, they strive to satisfy both of them at once. They imagine a unique power, tutelary, all-powerful, but elected by the citizens. They combine centralization and the sovereignty of the people. That gives them some slack. They console themselves with being under guardianship, thinking that they themselves have chosen their guardians. Each individual suffers from being tied up, because he sees that it is not a man or a class, but the people themselves, who hold the end of the chain. In this system, the citizens leave dependence for a moment to indicate their master, and then return to it" (Alexis de Tocqueville, *On Democracy in America*, Volume II, Part IV, Chapter VI).

*

"Mass education was designed to turn independent farmers into docile and passive instruments of production. That was its first objective. And don't think that people didn't know about it. They knew about it and fought it. There was a lot of resistance to mass education for this reason. It was also understood by the elites. Emerson once said something about how you educate them to keep them from jumping down your throat. If you don't educate them, which is called education, they will take over - they, being what Alexander Hamilton called "the Great Beast," which is the people. The anti-democratic thrust of opinion in what are called democratic societies is simply ferocious" (Noam Chomsky).

The lie as a central weapon of professional politicians, the worst will govern

"Governments protect and reward men in proportion to the part they play in organizing lies" (Leo Tolstoy).

*

"One must lie like a devil, not timidly, not for a time, but boldly and always. Lie, my friends, lie, I will return it to you one day" (Voltaire "Letter to Thiriot", October 21, 1736).

*

"There is what we say and there is what we do. There is a vocabulary to be caught, and it is easy with a few words - liberty and national independence - to make oneself heard by fools"

66

(Bonaparte, autumn 1795, quoted by Henri Guillemin, television lecture no. 3/15 on Napoleon, "Un militaire abusif").

*

"It is necessary to speak peace and act war" (Bonaparte, quoted by Henri Guillemin).

*

"Properly analyzed, political liberty is an agreed-upon fable, imagined by the rulers to lull the ruled to sleep" (Napoleon, quoted in *The Spirit of Napoleon: Thoughts and Maxims from his Writings*, Collection XIX, 2016).

*

"Men are like rabbits: they catch each other by the ears" (a word attributed to Mirabeau - who knew a lot).

*

"The conscious and intelligent manipulation of the opinions and organized habits of the masses plays an important role in democratic societies. Those who manipulate this imperceptible social mechanism of an invisible government really run the country" Edward Bernays, *Propaganda*, 1928).

*

"In this day and age, everyone claims to be a democrat, without even exempting those who, through interest or prejudice, are the most implacable enemies of all democracy. The banker who has become rich in the dirty dealings of the Stock Exchange, and the subsidized orator who climbs to the supposedly national tribune to defend the most revolting monopolies, call themselves democrats; the newspaper which every day echoes aristocratic declamations and which turns with the most fury against liberty and equality calls itself a democrat" (Albert Laponneraye, *Lettre aux Prolétaires* (1833), quoted by Pierre Rosanvallon in his 1993 article on the origins of the word democracy).

*

"It is mainly, if not exclusively, by the gift of oratory that the leaders succeeded, at the origin of the labor movement, in gaining their supremacy over the masses. There is no crowd that is capable of escaping the aesthetic and emotional power of speech. The beauty of the speech suggests the mass, and the suggestion delivers it without resistance to the influence of the speaker. Now, what essentially characterizes democracy is precisely the ease with which it succumbs to the magic of the word. In the democratic regime, the born leaders are orators and journalists. [In democratic states, there is a conviction that only the gift of speech makes one fit to lead public affairs. The same can be said, and in an even more absolute way, of the great democratic parties" (Robert Michels, *Les Partis politiques. Essay on the oligarchic tendencies of democracies*, 1911).

*

"Jacques Ellul], who already in the first half of the last century taught that the foundation of the legal legitimization of political power (the popular will expressed by vote) is an objectively unattainable chimera, a ridiculous myth but very useful for governing, and well known as such in political and sociological circles. The reality of democratic systems is not in the will of a base guiding the decisions of the top, but in the will of the top to produce consensus, that is to say the acquiescence of the base to its decisions, and this notably thanks to the manipulation of information (censorship, distortions)" (Jacques Ellul, quoted by Marco Della Luna and Paolo Cioni, *Neuro-slaves. Techniques and*

68

psychopathologies of political, economic and religious manipulation, Macro Editions, Cesena (Italy), 2011).

*

"By means of ever more effective methods of mental manipulation, democracies will change their nature. The old picturesque forms - elections, parliaments, high courts of justice - will remain, but the underlying substance will be a new form of 'non-violent' totalitarianism. All the traditional names and slogans will remain exactly as they were in the good old days. Democracy and freedom will be the theme of every broadcast ... and every editorial, but ... the ruling oligarchy and its highly trained elite of soldiers, policemen, thought-makers, and mental manipulators will run everything and everyone as it sees fit.

*

"Political language is designed to make lies sound like truth, to make murder sound respectable, and to make what is nothing but hot air sound solid" (George Orwell).

*

"Of course, the people do not want war. That's natural and understandable. But after all, it is the leaders of the country who decide the policies. Whether it is a democracy, a fascist dictatorship, a parliament or a communist dictatorship, it will always be easy to get the people to follow. Whether or not they have a voice, the people can always be made to think like their leaders. It is easy. All you have to do is tell them that they are under attack, denounce the unpatriotic nature of the pacifists, and assure them that they are putting the country in danger. The techniques remain the same, whatever the country" (Hermann Goering, during the Nuremberg trial in 1946).

*

"The politician strives to dominate opinion... So he puts all his art into seducing it, dissimulating according to the time, affirming only opportunely [...] Finally, by a thousand intrigues and oaths, he has conquered it: it gives him the power. Now, will he act without pretending? But no! He must still please, convince the prince or the Parliament, flatter the passions, hold the interests in suspense" (Charles de Gaulle).

Relevance of the opinion (and necessary participation) of ordinary citizens

"There is an advantage for a democracy, in the sense in which we understand democracy par excellence today (I mean that in which the people are sovereign even of the laws), to do, so that the deliberative body functions better, what is done for the courts in oligarchies (a fine is imposed to make those whom we want to see sit sit, while popular regimes give a salary to the modest people (so that they will sit); and also to do the same with respect to assemblies. Deliberation will indeed be better if all deliberate in common, the people with the notables, the latter with the masses" (Aristotle, *Politics* IV, 14, 1298-b).

*

"Are we going to forget [...] that ignorance combined with wise restraint is more profitable than skill combined with capriciousness, and that in general cities are better governed by ordinary people than by men of more subtle minds? The latter always want to appear more intelligent than the laws [...]. Ordinary people, on the contrary [...] do not pretend to have more discernment than the laws. They are less able to criticize the arguments of an eloquent speaker, and when judging matters they are guided by common sense and not by the spirit of competition. This is how their politics generally have happy effects" (Thucydides, *La Guerre du Péloponnèse*, II, 37, in *Œuvres complètes*, Paris, Gallimard, "Bibliothèque de la Pléiade", 1964, quoted by Yves Sintomer, *Le pouvoir au peuple. Jurys citoyens, tirage au sort et démocratie participative*, Paris, La Découverte, 2007, p. 47).

*

"Otanes, at first, asked that one gives to the Persian people the care to direct its own affairs. In my opinion, he declared, the power should no longer belong to one man among us: this regime is neither pleasant nor good. [...] How can monarchy be a balanced government when it allows one man to do as he pleases, without being accountable? Give this power to the most virtuous man in existence, and you will soon see him change his attitude. His newfound wealth breeds in him a pride without measure, and envy is innate in the man: with these two vices there is nothing left in him but perversity; he madly commits crimes without number, drunk sometimes with pride, sometimes with envy. A tyrant, however, should ignore envy, he who has everything, but it is in his nature to prove the contrary to his fellow citizens. He feels a jealous hatred to see good people living day after day; only the worst rascals please him, he excels in welcoming slander. Supreme inconsistency: keep some measure in your praise, he resents not being flattered basely; flatter him basely, he resents it again as if it were sycophancy. But worst of all, I'll tell you: it overturns ancestral customs, it outrages women, it makes anyone die without trial. On the contrary, the popular regime (*archon plethos*) bears the most beautiful name: equality (*isonomia*); secondly, it does not commit any of the excesses of which a monarch is guilty: fate distributes the charges, the magistrate is accountable for his acts, any decision is brought before the people. So here is

71

my opinion: let us give up monarchy and put the people in power, because only the majority must count" (Herodotus, *The Inquiry*, c. 445 B.C.).

*

"Our Constitution is called democracy because power is in the hands not of a minority, but of the whole people" (attributed to Pericles, according to Thucydides).

*

"The quickest way to open the eyes of a people is to put each one individually in a position to judge for himself and in detail the object which he had until then only appreciated in broad outline" (Machiavelli, *Discourse on the first decadence of Titus Livius*, book I, chap. XLVII).

*

"People will ask me if I am a prince or a legislator to write about politics. I answer that I am not, and that is why I write about politics. If I were a prince or a legislator, I would not waste my time saying what to do; I would do it, or I would keep quiet. Born a citizen of a free State, and a member of the sovereign, however little influence my voice may have in public affairs, the right to vote in them is enough to impose on me the duty of learning about them: happy, whenever I meditate on governments, to always find in my research new reasons to love that of my country! (Jean-Jacques Rousseau, *The Social Contract* (1762), introduction to Book I).

*

"The freedom to say everything has no enemies except those who want to reserve the freedom to do everything. When it is permitted to say everything, the truth speaks for itself and its triumph is assured" (Jean-Paul Marat, *Les Chaînes de l'esclavage*).

*

"The work of the legislator is not complete when he has only made the people happy. Even when the people are happy, there is still much to be done. Institutions must complete the moral education of citizens. By respecting their individual rights, by sparing their independence, by not disturbing their occupations, they must nevertheless consecrate their influence on public affairs, call upon them to contribute, by their decisions and by their votes, to the exercise of power, guarantee them a right of control and supervision through the expression of their opinions, and in this way train them by practice in these high functions, give them both the desire and the ability to carry them out" (Benjamin Constant, *De la liberté des Anciens comparée à celle des Modernes*, 1819)

Against inequalities

"This disposition to admire, and almost to venerate, the rich and powerful, as well as to despise, or at least to neglect, the poor and lowly, though necessary both to establish and to maintain the distinction of rank and order in society, is at the same time the greatest and most universal cause of the corruption of our moral sentiments. The moralists of all ages have complained that wealth and greatness are often looked upon with the respect and admiration due only to wisdom and virtue; and that contempt, of which vice and folly are the only proper objects, is often very unjustly attached to poverty and weakness" (Adam Smith, *Theory of Moral Sentiments*, 1759).

*

"If you want to give the State consistency, bring the extremes as close together as possible; suffer neither the wealthy nor the poor. These two states, which are naturally inseparable, are equally harmful to the common good; from one come the authors of tyranny, and from the other the tyrants: it is always between them that the traffic in public liberty takes place: the one buys it, and the other sells it" (Jean-Jacques Rousseau, *On the Social Contract* (1762), book II, chap. XI: "On the various systems of legislation").

*

"In trading nations, with capitalists and rentiers almost all in common cause with traders, financiers, and agioteurs, the great cities contain only two classes of citizens, one of whom vegetates in misery, and the other of whom abounds in superfluities: the latter possesses all the means of oppression; the former lacks all the means of defense. Thus, in republics, the extreme inequality of fortunes puts the entire people under the yoke of a handful of individuals" (Jean-Paul Marat, *Les Chaînes de l'esclavage*).

*

"The reasoning thus makes it obvious, it seems, that the sovereignty of a minority or a majority is only an accident, peculiar either to oligarchies or to democracies, due to the fact that everywhere the rich are in the minority and the poor in the majority. Therefore, the real difference between democracy and oligarchy is poverty and wealth; and necessarily, a regime where the rulers, whether they are in the minority or in the majority, exercise power thanks to their wealth is an oligarchy, and one where the poor rule, a democracy" (Aristotle, *Politics* III, 1279b34-1280a4, trans. Aubonnet, quoted by Moses I. Finley, *Ancient Democracy and Modern Democracy*, 1972, p. 58).

*

"Cursed be you, you are a coward, as are all those who accept to be governed by the laws that rich men have written to ensure their own security. They make us look like bandits, those villains, when there is only one difference between them and us, they rob the poor under the cover of the law while we rob the rich under the protection of our courage alone" (Charles Bellamy, quoted in Marcus Rediker, *Pirates of All Countries*, Montreuil, ed. Libertalia, 2008, reissued in paperback 2017).

Elections, or how to elect masters instead of laws

"Great men call shame the fact of losing and not that of deceiving to win" (Nicolas Machiavelli).

*

"The people, subject to the laws, must be the author of them; it belongs only to those who associate to regulate the conditions of society" (Jean-Jacques Rousseau, *Du contrat social ou Principes du droit politique* (1762), book II, chap. VI: "De la loi").

*

"Once a people has entrusted to some of its members the dangerous deposit of public authority and has given them the responsibility of enforcing the laws, always chained by them, sooner or later it sees its freedom, its property, its life at the mercy of the leaders it has chosen to defend it" (Jean-Paul Marat, *Les Chaînes de l'esclavage*).

*

"It is a political blasphemy to dare to advance that the nation, from which all powers emanate, can only exercise them by delegation; which would put it itself in the dependence, or rather under the yoke of its own representatives" (Jean-Paul Marat, 1791).

*

"If the bourgeois took up arms in '89, it was above all out of fear of the poor. The bourgeoisie used the poor they needed to intimidate the Court and to establish their own oligarchy. And the new masters, the Legislative, are businessmen for whom liberty is the privilege of getting rich without hindrance" (Jean-Paul Marat, *L'Ami du peuple*, November 20, 1791, *in* Henri Guillemin in *1789-1792 / 1792-1794, les deux Révolutions françaises*, Lacajunte (Landes), éd. Utovie, 2013, p. 110).

*

"The parliament, under the influence of the court, will never concern itself with public happiness. Don't you understand that intriguers who owe their appointment only to the gold they have sown, not content with neglecting your interests, make it their duty to treat you as vile mercenaries? Seeking to hang up what they have spent to corrupt you, they will only use the powers you have given them, to enrich themselves at your expense, to tamper with your rights with impunity" (Jean-Paul Marat, *Les Chaînes de l'esclavage*).

*

"Ballots, destined to be blown away by the wind with the promises of candidates, are no better than assegais against cannons. Do you think, citizens, that the rulers would let you have them if you could use them to make a revolution?" (Louise Michel, *Prise de possession*, 1890).

*

"The voter is one who enjoys the sacred privilege of voting for the man chosen by another" (Ambrose Gwinnett Bierce, 1880).

*

"Today the candidate bows to you, and perhaps too low; tomorrow he will straighten up and perhaps too high. He begs for votes, he will give you orders. [...] Does not the fiery democrat learn to bend his back when the banker deigns to invite him to his office, when the servants of kings do him the honor of entertaining him in the antechambers? The atmosphere of these legislative bodies is unhealthy to breathe; you send your representatives into an environment of corruption; do not be surprised if they come out corrupted [...] Instead of entrusting your interests to others, defend them yourselves; act!" (Élisée Reclus, "Letter to Jean Grave", *Le Révolté*, October 11, 1885).

*

"Can one speak of universal suffrage without laughing? All are obliged to recognize that it is a bad weapon [...] Your vote, it is the prayer to the deaf gods of all mythologies, something like the roar of an ox sniffing the slaughterhouse" (Louise Michel, *Prise de possession*, 1890).

*

"When you see universal suffrage and the people it gives us up close, you want to machine-gun the people and guillotine their representatives" (Guy de Maupassant, c. 1887).

*

"Paris! The Paris that votes, the mob, the sovereign people every four years... The people sufficiently stupid to believe that sovereignty consists in naming themselves masters. As if parked in front of the town halls, they were herds of voters, dazed, fetishists who held the little ballot paper with which they say: "I abdicate". [Add up the blank ballots and count the void ballots, add to them the abstentions, voices and silences that normally come together to signify either disgust or contempt. A bit of statistics please, and you will easily see that, in all the constituencies, the gentleman fraudulently proclaimed deputy does not have a quarter of the votes. Hence, for the purposes of the cause, this imbecile expression: relative majority - you might as well say that, at night, it is relatively light. Also the incoherent, the brutal Universal Suffrage which rests only on the number - and does not have even for him the number - will perish in the ridicule" (Alphonse Gallaud de la Pérouse, known as Zo d' Axa, *The Leaves, it is elected*, 1900).

*

"But what is an election really? The expression of the popular will, they say. Is it? We walk into a voting booth, and on a piece of paper, we draw a cross in front of one, two, maybe three or four names. Have we expressed what we think about U.S. policy? We probably have some ideas about it, with lots of "buts" and "ifs" and "buts". This cross on a piece of paper obviously says nothing. It would take us hours to express our ideas: to call a ballot an expression of our opinion is an empty fiction" (Walter Lippmann, 1927).

*

"To represent means to have accepted as the will of the mass what is only an individual will. It is possible to represent, in certain isolated cases, when it is a question, for example, of questions having clear and simple contours and when, moreover, the delegation is of short duration. But a permanent representation will always be equivalent to a hegemony of the representatives over the represented" (Robert Michels, *Les Partis politiques. Essay on the oligarchic tendencies of democracies*, 1911, p. 21).

*

"Many forms of government have been tested, and will be tested in this world of sin and evil. No one claims that democracy is perfect or omniscient. Indeed, it has been said to be the worst form of government except for all those that have been tried over time; but there is a feeling, widely shared in our country, that the people should be sovereign, continuously sovereign, and that public opinion, expressed by all constitutional means, should shape, guide, and control the actions of ministers who are its servants and not its masters. [... A group of men who have control of the machinery and a parliamentary majority have undoubtedly the power to propose what they want without the slightest regard to whether the people like it or not, or the slightest reference to its presence in their campaign program. [...] Is the opposing party really to be allowed to pass laws affecting the very character of this country in the last years of this Parliament without any appeal to the right of the people to vote, who have placed them where they are? No, sir, democracy says, "No, a thousand times no. You do not have the right to pass laws in the last phase of a legislature that are not accepted and desired by the popular majority. (Winston Churchill, speech of November 11, 1947).

*

"Long before the German electorate brought Hitler to power, when Bonaparte (Napoleon III) had murdered the republic, he proclaimed universal suffrage. When Count Bismarck had secured the victory of the Prussian hoberels, he proclaimed universal suffrage. In both cases, the proclamation, the granting of universal suffrage sealed the triumph of despotism. This alone should open the eyes of lovers of universal suffrage" (Wilhelm Liebknecht).

Arguments for the draw

"But constitutions change even without sedition, due to intrigues alone, as in Heria, where elections were replaced by the drawing of lots because it was intriguers who were elected, or due to negligence when enemies of the constitution are allowed to reach the most important magistracies [...]" (Aristotle, *Politics* book V, chap. III, 1303a).

*

"In a democracy, the desire to limit the power of magistrates is combined with the desire to have everyone serve in turn as a magistrate. Rotation is ensured in part by multiplying the number of posts as much as possible: if, as a result, a very large proportion of the civic population is destined to hold office sooner or later, drawing lots is the logical way to achieve this. Even in a democracy, certain prestigious and advantageous offices are more coveted: the drawing of lots ensures that the question of who will obtain them will be settled by chance, whereas election opens the field to quarrels and, in the last analysis, to *stásis* [civil unrest]: the democrats preferred the drawing of lots because it prevented corruption and divisions in the civic body" (Mogens Herman Hansen, *La Démocratie athénienne à l'époque de Démosthène, Structure, principes et idéologie*, Paris, Les Belles Lettres, 1993, p. (Mogens Herman Hansen, La Démocratie athénienne époque Démosthène, Structure, principes et idéologie, Paris, Les Belles Lettres, 1993, p. 275, quoted by Fabrice Wolff, *Qu'est-ce que la démocratie directe ? (Manifeste pour une comédie historique)*, Éditions Antisociales, 2010).

*

"Democracy: a form of government where offices are given by lot" (César-Pierre Richelet, *Dictionnaire français*, Geneva, 1680).

80

*

"Suffrage by lot is of the nature of democracy; suffrage by choice is of the nature of aristocracy. The lot is a way of electing which does not afflict anyone; it leaves to each citizen a reasonable hope of serving his country. But, since it is defective in itself, it is in regulating and correcting it that the great legislators have surpassed themselves. Solon established in Athens that all military posts would be appointed by choice, and that senators and judges would be elected by lot. He wanted that the civil magistracies which required a great expenditure were given by choice, and that the others were given by the lot. But, to correct the lot, he regulated that one could elect only in the number of those which would be presented; that that which would have been elected would be examined by judges, and that each one could accuse him of being unworthy of it: that held at the same time of the lot and the choice. When the time of one's magistracy was over, one had to undergo another judgment on the manner in which one had behaved. People without capacity must have been very reluctant to give their name to be drawn by lot" (Montesquieu, *De l'esprit des lois*, book II, chapter II).

*

"It is difficult to conceive how men who have entirely renounced the habit of governing themselves could succeed in choosing well those who should lead them; and it will not be believed that a liberal, energetic and wise government could ever emerge from the suffrages of a people of servants" (Alexis de Tocqueville, *On Democracy in America*, volume II, part four, chapter VI).

*

"All conformisms, in the broad sense, are by nature more unconscious. From this point of view, the drawing of lots ensures the diversity of choices and, even more than neutrality, it is a general form of impartiality and a source of richness in the expression of personalities and the development of behaviors. On the contrary, the very elaborate and codified rules of co-optation generally push to standardize choices" (Gil Delannoi, *Le retour du tirage au sort en politique*, Fondapol, 2010).

About the constituent process

"The people, when they make magistrates, must create them in such a way that they have every reason to fear severe justice, if they were to abuse their power" (Nicolas Machiavelli, *Discourse on the first decadence of Titus Livius*, book I, chapter XLI).

*

"Before examining the act by which a people elects a king, therefore, it would be well to examine the act by which a people is a people; for this act, being necessarily prior to the other, is the true foundation of society. Indeed, if there were no prior convention, where would be, unless the election were unanimous, the obligation for the few to submit to the choice of the many? and from where do a hundred who want a master have the right to vote for ten who do not? The law of the plurality of votes is itself an establishment of convention and presupposes unanimity at least once" (Jean-Jacques Rousseau, *Du contrat social ou Principes du droit politique* (1762), book I, chap. V: "That it is always necessary to go back to a first convention").

*

"All constitutions, all laws, naturally expire after a period of nineteen years. To maintain their empire after this term is an act of force and not of right" (Thomas Jefferson to James Madison, Paris, September 6, 1789).

*

"Most legislators have been narrow-minded men, whom chance has put in charge of others, and who have consulted almost only their own prejudices and fancies. It seems that they have disregarded the very greatness and dignity of their work: they have amused themselves by making puerile institutions, with which they have, to be sure, conformed to small minds, but have discredited themselves in the eyes of people of good sense. They have thrown themselves into useless details; they have given themselves over to particular cases, which is the mark of a narrow-minded genius that sees things only in parts, and does not embrace anything from a general view. Some of them have tried to use a language other than the common one: an absurd thing for a law-maker. How can they be observed if they are not known? They have often abolished without necessity those which they have found established; that is to say, they have thrown the people into the disorders inseparable from changes. It is true that, by a quirk that comes rather from nature than from the minds of men, it is sometimes necessary to change certain laws. But the case is rare, and, when it happens, it should only be touched with a trembling hand: so many solemnities must be observed and so many precautions taken that the people naturally conclude that the laws are quite holy, since so many formalities are needed to abrogate them [...]" (Montesquieu, *Lettres persanes* (1721, reedited 1754), letter CXXIX "Usbek to Rhedi *in Venice*", Paris, Le Livre de Poche, 1967, p. 327 ff).

*

"What is sovereign, in fact, is force, which is always in the hands of a small fraction of the nation. What must be sovereign is justice. All political constitutions, republican and otherwise, have as their sole end - if they are legitimate - to prevent or at least to limit the oppression to which force naturally inclines. And when there is oppression, it is not the nation that is oppressed. It is a man, and a man, and a man. The nation does not exist; how could it be sovereign? These empty formulas have done too much harm for us to be indulgent" (Simone Weil, "Remarques sur le nouveau projet de Constitution", in *Écrits de Londres et dernières lettres*, Paris, Gallimard, "Espoir", 1957).

*

"Any man who has the power to bully or deceive men must be obliged to make a commitment not to do so" (Simone Weil, "Remarks on the new draft constitution", in *Écrits de Londres et dernières lettres, op. cit.*).

Legitimacy

"The strongest is never strong enough to be always the master, if he does not transform his strength into right, and obedience into duty" (Jean-Jacques Rousseau, *On the Social Contract*, book I, chap. III: "On the right of the strongest").

*

"What makes the state one? It is the union of its members. And from where is the union of its members born? From the obligation that binds them. All is agreed so far. But what is the basis of this obligation? Here is where the authors are divided. According to some, it is force; according to others, paternal authority; according to others, the will of God. Each one establishes his own principle and attacks that of the others: I myself have not done otherwise, and, following the healthiest part of those who have discussed these matters, I have established the agreement of its members as the foundation of the body politic, and I have refuted the principles that differ from mine.

84

Independently of the truth of this principle, it prevails over all others by the solidity of the foundation it establishes; for what surer foundation can obligation have among men than the free commitment of the one who obliges himself? Any other principle can be disputed [...]; this one cannot be disputed" (Jean-Jacques Rousseau, *Lettres écrites de la montagne*, 1764, sixth letter).

*

"Originally, kings and princes were all simple brigand leaders" (Jean-Paul Marat, *Les Chaînes de l'esclavage*).

*

"There is a paradox of power, for power is fear in action, and fear is contagious: it is impossible to frighten men without ending up being frightened of them. It is from this law of the human spirit that the greatest torment of life is born: the mutual fear of power and its subjects. To combat this scourge, humanity has so far found only two remedies: first, mystical philosophies and religions; second, in recent centuries, the principles of legitimacy. In short, a legitimate government is a power that has freed itself from fear, because it has learned to rely on consent, active or passive, and to reduce the use of force in proportion" (Guglielmo Ferrero, *Power. Les génies invisibles de la cité* (1942, posthumous), Paris, Le Livre de Poche, 1988).

Common good, general interest, need for controversy

"What is just is what is appropriate to the common good" (Claude Rochet, according to Saint Thomas Aquinas).

*

"The criterion of good can only be truth, justice and, secondly, public utility. Democracy, the power of the greatest

85

number, are not goods. They are means to the good, rightly or wrongly considered effective. Only what is just is legitimate" (Simone Weil, "Note sur la suppression générale des partis politiques", in *Écrits de Londres et dernières lettres, op. cit.*).

*

"What must be safeguarded above all, what is the priceless good conquered by man through all the prejudices, all the sufferings and all the struggles, is this idea that there is no sacred truth, that is to say, one that is forbidden to the full investigation of man; it is what is greatest in the world, it is the sovereign liberty of the spirit; it is that no power, either internal or external, no power, no dogma, must limit the perpetual effort and the perpetual research of the human race [ ]; it is that any truth that does not come from us is a lie" (Christopher Hill, *The English Revolution 1640*, Paris, Les Éditions de la Passion, 1993).

*

"In Japan, in the early seventh century, the Buddhist prince Shokoto…was also the originator of a relatively liberal constitution or Kempo, called the "Constitution of the 17 Articles. Very much in the spirit of the *Magna* Carta signed six centuries later in England, it insisted that decisions on matters of importance should not be made by one person alone. They should be discussed by several people. The constitution also advised: "Let us not be inclined to resent when the opinions of others differ from our own. For every man has a heart, and every heart has its own inclinations. What is right for some is wrong for others, and vice versa" (Amartya Sen, *The Democracy of Others. Why freedom is not an invention of the West*, Paris, Payot, "Manuels Payot", 2005, p. 32).

*

"A conviction is only strengthened if we feed it with objections" (Nicolás Gómez Dávila, *The Horrors of Democracy*, Monaco, Éditions du Rocher, 2003).

*

"The same people who took away their eyes reproach the people for being blind" (John Milton, quoted by Noam Chomsky, *La fabrication du consentement. De la propagande médiatique en démocratie*, Marseille, Agone, 2008).

Tyranny

"The accumulation of all powers, legislative, executive, and judicial, in the same hands, either of one man, or of a few, or of many, either by heredity, by conquest, or by election, may justly be considered as the true definition of tyranny" (James Madison, *The Federalist*, No. 47, February 1, 1788).

*

"Thus, the last blow that princes strike against liberty is to violate the laws in the name of the laws themselves, to overthrow them all, pretending to defend them, and to punish as a rebel anyone who dares to defend them in fact: the cruelest tyranny of all, in that it is exercised under the very cloak of justice" (Jean-Paul Marat, *The Chains of Slavery*).

*

"If in the interior of a State you do not hear the sound of any conflict, you can be sure that freedom is not there" (Montesquieu).

*

"Despotism, that form of government where no one is a citizen" (Montesquieu).

*

"All would be lost, if the same man, or the same body of principals, or nobles, or people, exercised these three powers: that of making laws, that of executing public resolutions, and that of judging the crimes or disputes of individuals" (Montesquieu, *De l'esprit des lois*, book XI: "Of the laws which form political liberty in its relation to the constitution", chap. VI: "Of the constitution of England").

*

"Moreover, citizens do not allow themselves to be oppressed except insofar as, driven by blind ambition, and looking more below than above them, domination becomes more dear to them than independence, and they consent to wear irons in order to be able to give some in their turn. It is very difficult to reduce to obedience those who do not seek to command, and the most skilful politician would not be able to subjugate men who would only want to be free. But inequality spreads easily among ambitious and cowardly souls, always ready to run the risks of fortune, and to dominate or serve almost indifferently according to whether it becomes favourable or contrary to them" (Jean-Jacques Rousseau, *Discourse on the Origin of Inequality Among Men* (1754), second part, Paris, Éditions Garnier Frères, 1962, p. 87-88).

*

"A constitution must be short and obscure. It must be made in such a way as not to hinder the action of the government" (attributed to Napoleon Bonaparte).

*

"Any leader will be a detestable tyrant if he is allowed to do so" (Alain).

*

"The powerful have no more vital interest than to prevent this crystallization of the submissive crowds, or at least, because they cannot always prevent it, to make it as rare as possible. That the same emotion agitates at the same time a great number of unhappy people, which happens very often by the natural course of things; but usually this emotion, hardly awakened, is repressed by the feeling of an irremediable impotence. To maintain this feeling of powerlessness is the first article of a skillful policy on the part of the masters" (Simone Weil, "Meditation on Obedience and Freedom", in *Oppression and Freedom* (1934), Paris, Gallimard, "Espoir", 1955).

*

"Parties are a marvelous mechanism, by virtue of which, throughout a country, not a single mind gives its attention to the effort of discerning, in public affairs, the good, justice, and truth [...] By this triple character, every party is totalitarian in germ and in aspiration. If it is not totalitarian in fact, it is only because those who surround it are no less totalitarian than it" (Simone Weil, "Note sur la suppression générale des partis politiques", in *Écrits de Londres et dernières lettres, op. cit.*).

*

"The very names of the four ministries that lead us show a kind of impudence in the deliberate reversal of facts. The Ministry of Peace deals with war, the Ministry of Truth deals with lies, the Ministry of Love deals with torture, the Ministry of Abundance deals with famine. These contradictions are not accidental, nor are they the result of ordinary hypocrisy, they are deliberate exercises in doublethink. It is indeed only by reconciling opposites that power can be indefinitely retained. The old cycle could not be broken in any other way. For human equality to be forever removed, for the great, as we have called them, to perpetually hold their places, the prevailing mental condition must be directed madness" (George Orwell, *1984*).

8.
Conclusion
The nice surprise of Christmas 2018:
the "yellow vests" show us the way

For fourteen years (since 2005), I have been reading in all directions everything related to powers, abuses of power and institutions: history, law, economics, political philosophy, sociology, anthropology, from the Bible to the present day, everything interests me, as long as it gives me ideas and strength to organize the resistance of human beings to all systems of domination. I try to understand how we arrived at the unjust and violent world we have, and how we could (really) improve life on earth. Every time I find a book, a thesis, an idea, a fact, a proof, an intellectual, a text, a video, or any document that seems useful to understand and resist the abuses of power, I post it on my site and we talk about it together. Thus, I have exposed tens of thousands of links to the interest and criticism of citizens.

During these exciting years, I often found myself thinking that all this was not going to be enough, that the very rich were going to win the game, simply by giving the 99% the minimum comfort that puts us all to sleep, that anaesthetizes our conscience and our fighting spirit. I found most voters apathetic. It's clever to buy the biggest media to control them, and to distract the opinion from the essential problems. I despaired to see that people, decerebrated by TV commercials, are completely uninterested in their institutions.

And then the successive governments (of the right and the left) have amplified their "liberal" policies, accelerated the "reforms" (regressions) and aggravated the mistreatments in an indecent and exasperating way. The rich, who live in obscene luxury, have begun to attack our salaries and our pensions in order to gorge themselves more than ever. These governments of the rich for the rich have imposed a list as long as a day without bread of measures contrary to the general interest.... Our lack of reaction was to be despaired of.

And this fall of 2018, with the "yellow vests", despair has turned into hope: this movement of revolt, unitary, peaceful and radical, I have dreamed of it for ten years. These "yellow vests" are doing what we should all do. They are *exemplary* in many ways:

Exemplary, they leave their homes and they remake society

First, those who suffer come out of their homes and brave the cold, the rain and the night. Instead of staying cooped up, they get together to socialize. They realize that there are many of them and their shame turns to anger. They think about their most serious problems, traffic circle by traffic circle, tollgate by tollgate. Whether it rains or is cold, the "yellow vests" celebrate, cook their food and build huts, are happy to come back to the traffic circle and find a new family... They remain united, pacifist, determined and imagine a better world. They go out and rebuild their society. These are civic schools: the free commune of the Pont de l'Étoile tollbooth, the free commune of the

Saint-Clair-sur-Rhône traffic circle, the free commune of the La Bouilladisse crossroads… It is exceptional, this return to the original spirit of the commune: we must relearn how to manage the common together.

So, the first exemplary point: they leave their homes as we should leave our homes and go to public places as we should go to public places, and they stay there stubbornly as we should stay there stubbornly, despite the cold, despite the wind, despite the rain. This is totally unprecedented. Usually, social movements happen in spring and we go home as soon as it rains.

Exemplary, they rethink the rules of representation before designating their representatives

And that's not all: disgusted by decades of lies from politicians, whether "left" or "right" or "center", completely disgusted by the professionals of politics, they arrive at the traffic circles with a detestation of representation: *they don't want representatives*, they don't want to hear about "politics".

In my opinion, when they say this, they are talking about "politicians", and they don't realize that their movement is deeply political in the best sense of the word: they are concerned (as we all should be too) with the decisions that should be made for the common good.

In particular, *they think about the rules of representation BEFORE appointing representatives*: on our traffic circle, which representatives do we want? Masters? Servants? Out of control? Controlled (how?) and revocable at any time? Which mandate(s)? What duration? Renewable? They think about it for their traffic circle, as we should think about it for our society.

For example, see this building site constituting a place of occupation of yellow vests in Tonneins (dpt 47) :

Proposal of articles to represent a group more or less vast (traffic circle or region...) :	Your own ideas (criticisms and proposals) for political adults:
Art. 1 : the spokesmen, called mandataries, are freely designated by each represented (citizen) who deposits a name (his own name if he is a candidate, or if not, the name of another, candidate or not) in a hat, from where will be drawn x mandataries. Art. 2 : the represented (citizens) give a mandate of representation to the representatives and substitutes, for a period of x days, after a preparation session (briefing) at the end of which they are entrusted with a mission (either to vote in our place, or to prepare our vote) from which they cannot deviate (imperative mandate) Art. 3: The representatives and their substitutes may only exercise their representation filmed, recorded and broadcast live by all necessary means. Art. 4: The representatives and their substitutes can be revoked immediately and at any time, at the request of x represented (citizens) on the ICR website. Art. 5: At the end of the mission, the representatives report (debriefing) to the represented (citizens), who can then give them discharge (approval) or not.	

Exemplary, they insist on remaining united

And that's not all: the yellow vests know very well that there are people from the left and the right among them, and they are very careful that no one says so, that no one has a flag or a banner of the left or the right to wave. This is both historic and decisive. The first historical point is that this is a UNITARY movement.

What prevents the people from winning is the divisions, the zizanie on legislative subjects (by essence conflicting: it is normal and legitimate to argue on legislative subjects), on subjects on which we are used to discuss whereas we have however strictly no power of decision: it is not us who decide, it is the elected representatives. We are used to arguing for nothing because, in any case, it is not us who decide. The central idea of the "yellow vests" is: *no zizanie, let's stay united.*

Exemplary, they first reflect on important, but mainly legislative grievances

Ten days were enough for them to draw up a list of remarkable grievances: no more homeless, social security for all, a minimum wage of 1,300 euros... "Grievances" are requests to a master, requests made by an inferior being to a superior being, because that is what it comes down to: there are superior beings who are "the elected" and inferior beings who are the voters. Accustomed to this situation of submission, the voters, in relation to the elected, like all the peoples of the world at the moment when they revolt, demand decisions at the *legislative level* (which it is essential to distinguish from the *constituent* level) such as: "we want better salaries, we want less taxes, we want less waste, less privileges for the elected, less destruction of public services, etc."

List of grievances of the yellow vests (November 2018):

- Zero homelessness: URGENT.
- More progressivity in income tax, i.e. more brackets.
- smic to 1,300 euros nct.

- Favour small businesses in villages and town centers. Stop the construction of big commercial zones around the big cities which kill the small trade and more free parking in the city centers.

- Large plan of insulation of the residences to make ecology by making savings with the households.

- Taxes: let the BIG ones (MacDo, Google, Amazon, Carrefour...) pay BIG and let the small ones (craftsmen, VSE, SME) pay small.

- Same social security system for all (including artisans and self-employed). End of the RSI.

- The pension system must remain based on solidarity and therefore socialized. No points-based retirement.

- End of fuel tax increase.

- No pension below 1,200 euros.

- All elected representatives will be entitled to the median salary. Transportation expenses will be monitored and reimbursed if justified. Entitlement to luncheon vouchers and vacation vouchers.

- The salaries of all French people as well as pensions and benefits must be indexed to inflation.

- Protecting French industry: banning relocation. Protecting our industry means protecting our know-how and our jobs.

- End of posted work. It is abnormal that a person who works on French territory does not benefit from the same salary and the same rights. Any person authorized to work on French territory must be on an equal footing with a French citizen and his employer must contribute to the same level as a French employer.

- For job security: further limit the number of fixed-term contracts for large companies. We want more permanent contracts.

- End of the CICE. Use this money to launch a French hydrogen car industry (which is truly ecological, unlike the electric car).

- End of the austerity policy. We stop paying back the interest on the debt, which has been declared illegitimate, and we start paying back the debt without taking money from the poor and less poor, but by going after the 80 billion in tax evasion.

- *That the causes of forced migration be addressed.*
- *That asylum seekers are treated well. We owe them housing, security, food and education for minors. Work with the UN to open reception camps in many countries of the world, pending the outcome of the asylum application.*
- *That rejected asylum seekers be returned to their country of origin.*
- *That a real integration policy be implemented. Living in France implies becoming French (French language course, French history course and civic education course with a certification at the end of the course).*
- *Maximum salary set at 15,000 euros.*
- *That jobs are created for the unemployed.*
- *Increase in disabled benefits.*
- *Rent controls. More low-cost housing (especially for students and precarious workers).*
- *Prohibition to sell the goods belonging to France (dam, airport…)*
- *Substantial resources for the justice system, the police, the gendarmerie and the army. That the overtime of the forces of order be paid or recovered.*
- *All the money earned from freeway tolls will have to be used for the maintenance of France's freeways and roads as well as for road safety.*
- *Since the price of gas and electricity has increased since privatization, we want them to become public again and the prices to drop significantly.*
- *Immediate end to the closure of short lines, post offices, schools and maternity wards.*
- *Let's bring well-being to our elderly. No more making money off the elderly. The white gold is over. The era of grey gold has begun.*
- *Maximum 25 students per class from kindergarten to 12th grade.*
- *Substantial resources provided to psychiatry.*
- *The popular referendum must be included in the Constitution. Creation of a readable and efficient site, supervised by an*

independent control body, where people can make a law proposal. If this bill obtains 700,000 signatures, it will have to be discussed, completed and amended by the National Assembly, which will be obliged (one year to the day after obtaining 700,000 signatures) to submit it to a vote of the entire French population.

- *Return to a 7-year term for the President of the Republic. The election of deputies two years after the election of the President of the Republic would allow to send a positive or negative signal to the President of the Republic concerning his policy. This would help to make the voice of the people heard.*
- *Retirement at age 60 and, for all those who have worked in a profession that wears out the body (bricklayer or boner for example), the right to retire at age 55.*
- *A child of 6 years old not being looked after alone, continuation of the Pajemploi system until the child is 10 years old.*
- *Promote the transport of goods by rail.*
- *No withholding tax.*
- *End of lifetime presidential allowances.*
- *Prohibition of tax on merchants when their customers use credit cards. Tax on marine fuel and kerosene.*

Source (for example): http://www.gaucherepublicaine.org/respublica/les-revendications-des-gilets-jaunes-un-vrai-cahier-de-doleances/7402768

Their demands are well formulated and they are (almost) all of a *legislative* nature, that is to say that, in order for them to be satisfied, our masters must agree to them and pass the corresponding laws. The universal problem is that these elected masters are not going to give everything: they, who have served us so poorly up to now, are obviously not going to start serving us properly at the first demonstration that comes along: they are going to satisfy one or two grievances, but certainly not all forty.

Appearance of the RIC: a constituent pearl in the middle of a list of legislative grievances

And, a major historical point, the "yellow vests" do not list only grievances. Every time there are revolts on earth, the damned of the earth insurgents demand new laws that are less cruel to them; that is ordinary, that is usual. But what is extraordinary is that in the list of grievances of the French yellow vests, there is a kind of gem, like a star in the sky, which is called the referendum of citizen initiative (RIC).

Why is the ICR so valuable?

The ICR is valuable because it is not legislative at all, but constitutive: it is not a matter of saying "this is a law we want", it is a matter of saying "this is how we want to write the laws, ourselves". This is extremely subversive - unstoppable and universal. It is radically democratic.

Exemplary, they make ICR in all matters a priority

When I saw the RIC in the list of grievances of the GJ, I obviously noticed that it was something very important. This line is quite different: if we get that, we'll have everything else, and even much more, and sustainably. We will have the means to vote ourselves the laws that we find important. So this is worth making a priority, because if we ask for forty different things, even if there are a lot of us, the force of each demand will be weak. And the elected officials will only need to grant us two or three of those requests to get rid of us and send us home. Instead, if we turn those forty petitions into two petitions, one on the citizens' referendum that will give us access to everything else, and a second one on a targeted financial aspect (so that the poorest people stop suffering so much right away), if we concentrate our efforts, we will have much more strength to access popular sovereignty outright, instead of getting only crumbs as usual. That's what they did.

And so, the idea of the yellow vests is not only to include the RIC in their list of grievances, but also to make it a priority. Then, all the yellow vests and, I hope, soon the *non-yellow vests*, will push together two decisive demands so that the misery of the poor will stop and so that popular power will finally come with a true RIC, to perforate the system of domination.

It's very spectacular that they managed to do that. They are already focusing on the RIC, it's quite magnificent: the yellow vests have understood this idea very quickly and it is spreading very, very fast.

Exemplary, the yellow vests know that they must learn to establish their power themselves

The yellow vests are discovering this essential fact: if we don't have the RIC, it's not because it's impossible, it's because those who write constitutions have a personal interest in our not having it. Our masters, our elected officials, do not want us to have the ICR and they will never want it. They want to decide everything and the solution will not come from them.

The yellow vests are already doing constituent workshops to write themselves the rules of a real RIC. This preparation for a popular constituent process is a second and quite historic point (the first point is the fierce will to remain united). The #GiletsJaunesConstituents pass the word among themselves, they know that the rich and the elected are lying when they say they are going to give them a RIC, while they are going to give them a fake RIC. The yellow vests, not fooled, are writing the RIC they want, that is to say *in all matters, without safeguards, without limits, without prohibitions*. With this true RIC, we will be able to impose a law, to abrogate a law or a treaty, to dismiss a political actor - any political actor, elected magistrate or high civil servant -, and then to modify the Constitution itself, *if we judge it useful.* Hey, that's sovereignty! Didn't I dream it?

The Constitutional Council must not be allowed to stand in the way of popular sovereignty. We recall that this body, which is not subject to citizen control, is composed of a bunch of old oligarchs who are corrupt to the core, that it receives multinationals in secret (cf. the "narrow doors" scandal) and that it now blocks all laws of general interest against cartels. There is no question of a Constitutional Council, composed of anyone, hindering popular sovereignty. This Council has no political legitimacy: it was imposed by an anti-Constitution that was voted under the military threat of a coup. I recall that, when de Gaulle had the Fifth Republic voted, it was under the threat of a military putsch that was taking shape in Corsica. Moreover, all those who wrote and accepted this anti-constitution are now dead, or almost. It is unacceptable that the dead govern the living. Condorcet said very well: "A generation cannot subject future generations to its laws". The institution of the Constitutional Council, by its very composition, is illegitimate. This can be the subject of a debate, but I can tell you that these are discussions that are circulating among the yellow vests.

Nor, of course, should the media be controlled by nine billionaires, as they are today: in a democracy, citizens' opinions must be fully and honestly informed before they vote. The appropriation of all the newspapers of the country allows the richest to intoxicate the opinion and to lead the citizens, badly informed, to vote *against* their own interests. So a real RIC in the current media situation would be downright dangerous. Hence the drafting by the Yellow Vests of ICR articles establishing *the independence of all information media: newspapers, televisions, radios, press agencies, polling institutes and statistical institutes.* See the example in the box below.

We have identified two techniques (but there are surely others, appeal to the population) to make journalists independent: either we make them personal owners of their media and forbid anyone to buy a media; or we make journalists independent civil servants of all powers, like judges are - but better because, if we write these articles, we will better separate powers and provide for *Chambers of Control drawn by lot* to evaluate the action (and engage the responsibility) of both judges and journalists who would abuse their power.

To understand with a concrete example what the yellow vests are working on with the RIC, and the extent of the political power they want to give themselves, here is one of the sites worked on the traffic circles:

In the constitution currently:

- 2 referendums at the initiative of the President or the Parliament.
- Nothing to the initiative of the people.

Copies of proposed amendments to the Constitution:

- A single referendum, of popular initiative (RIC), in all matters (ETM) and written by ourselves (EPNM)

Current Article 3:

National sovereignty belongs to the people, who exercise it through their representatives and through referendums.

Proposed Article 3:

National sovereignty belongs to the people, who exercise it through their representatives and by means of a citizens' initiative referendum, in all matters including constitutional matters and the ratification of treaties; this article can only be amended by referendum.

Current Article 11:

[Entry into force in accordance with the conditions laid down by the laws and organic laws necessary for their application (Article 46-I of Constitutional Act No. 2008-724 of 23 July 2008)]. The President of the Republic, on the proposal of the Government during the sessions or on the joint proposal of the two Assemblies, published in the Journal Officiel, may submit to a referendum any bill concerning the organization of the public powers, on reforms relating to the economic, social or environmental policy of the nation and to the public services that contribute to it, or tending to authorize the ratification of a treaty which, without being contrary to the Constitution, would have an impact on the functioning of the institutions.

When the referendum is organized on the proposal of the Government, the latter makes a statement before each assembly, which is followed by a debate.

A referendum on a subject mentioned in the first paragraph may be held on the <u>initiative of one fifth of the members of Parliament</u>, supported by one tenth of the electors registered on the electoral rolls. This initiative shall take the form of a bill and may not have as its object the repeal of a legislative provision promulgated less than one year ago.

The conditions of its presentation and those in which the Constitutional Council shall verify compliance with the provisions of the preceding paragraph shall be determined by an organic law.

If the bill has not been examined by the two assemblies within a time limit set by the organic law, the President of the Republic shall submit it to a referendum.

If the proposed law is not adopted by the French people, no new proposal for a referendum on the same subject may be presented before the expiry of a period of two years following the date of the vote.

When the referendum has resulted in the adoption of the bill or proposed law, the President of the Republic shall promulgate the law within fifteen days of the proclamation of the results of the consultation.

Section 11 deleted and replaced with:

Proposed Article 11:
PRACTICAL TERMS OF ICR:
TRIGGERING THRESHOLDS:

- The Referendum Chamber (drawn by lot) organizes the planning of referendums and controls the contradictory debates (the staging of conflicts) before any referendum, on the referendum website and on referendum television, in order to enlighten the opinion for at least 6 months before the vote. Four referendum celebrations are organized each year, which are public holidays, with pay.

- Any collective initiative that receives the support of 1% of the registered voters (400,000 voters) [or 0.5%] is automatically (unfiltered) included in the referendum calendar at least 6 months later.

- House-filtered individual initiative: A single citizen may present an initiative to the House of Referendums, which owes the citizen an hour's hearing (or more if the House deems it necessary) to explain the idea. The House then decides whether to reject the individual initiative or to place it on the referendum calendar.

- Individual initiative by increasing circles: any citizen can, by his own means, consult his fellow citizens.

- If the sample consulted (more than 1,000 people in the same locality, village, street, etc.) is favourable to the initiative, the municipality or municipalities of the citizens consulted must quickly organize a municipal referendum.

- If the municipal referendum is favourable to the initiative, the department to which the municipality belongs must promptly hold a departmental referendum.

- If the departmental referendum is favorable to the initiative, the nation must hold a national referendum.

- Any unfavorable outcome prior to reaching the national level will stop the initiative's progress.

DEADLINE AND ORGANIZATION OF CONTRADICTORY DEBATES
to inform opinion before the vote:

Any referendum must be preceded by a period of between three months and two years of full adversarial debate to inform public opinion. The Chamber of Referendums is responsible for the organization and quality control of these debates.

The opinion of the citizens must be honestly and completely informed in all circumstances. To this end, all media in the country (newspapers, radio, television, news agencies, polling and statistical institutes) must be owned by their journalists and employees at the time. No person, natural or legal, may buy any media. The current owners of the media must give them to their employees free of charge. The Media Chamber (drawn by lot) ensures that these rules are applied.

SELF-REINFORCING FORCE AND ABSENCE OF "CONTROL BODIES" (no possible blockade by a "Supreme Court" or "Constitutional Council"):

- Once the popular initiative has been passed by a majority, the Chamber of Referendums controls the honesty of the ballots and must declare the decision taken, without any body being able to oppose the popular will.

- A decision taken by RIC is superior to any other norm: regulations, laws, constitution or treaties; in France, country of free men, the people are sovereign, really.

Source : http://etienne.chouard.free.fr

It is a work in progress and you, the reader, are invited to correct it, to complete it... But beware, you are going to become a constituent and therefore a political adult. I do not guarantee that you will ever return to your previous state.

A substantial financial request for those who are starving

As for the second demand (financial), the yellow vests initially asked for an increase in the minimum wage, but they quickly realized that this measure would have the disadvantage of putting many very small businesses in great difficulty, which cannot bear an increase in the SMIC to 1,300 or 1,500 euros. They therefore changed their request. The problem to be solved is that there are people who are in a very cruel situation and who are hungry today. So there is a social emergency, and in order for people to stop being hungry, we can increase their income (the idea of an increased minimum wage), but we can also reduce by half the price of all the basic necessities, which constitute 100% of their basket. The idea, then, is that the yellow vests draw up a list of basic necessities: food products, clothing products, sanitary products, medicines, housing products, energy products, electricity, heating, etc. and ask only for a significant drop in their prices, but in an inflexible way. It is necessary to demand that the State abolish all taxes on these products and, since this will not be enough to lower prices significantly, it is also necessary to demand that the State *subsidize* prices in order to finally reduce them *by half*. Thus, since these products make up the entire basket of poor people, if these prices are halved, it is as if their wages were doubled.

And to put a figure on this, economists - and not the "economists" employed by banks who condemn us to austerity, but real economists who are friends of the people, such as the group of the *Dismayed Economists* - should calculate the approximate global cost of the state subsidy applied to all the basic products. Then we have to find the means to finance this measure, such as abolishing the CICE (tax credit for competitiveness and employment) in order to recover 40 billion per year of useless gifts to the rich. It is easy to find the few billions that will be necessary to allow the poor to suffer less.

An evolutionary rather than a revolutionary movement

So it's a question of instituting popular sovereignty, the real one, without oligarchic chains, and that's quite revolutionary. It is even more than *revolutionary* because to make a revolution is to make a complete turn, so we come back to the starting point and in fact we have only changed masters, most of the time. Most revolutions do not lead to emancipation. So it's more a matter of *evolution* than *revolution*, and a real evolution, a major one in the history of humanity: humans, so the constituent yellow vests and soon the others, those who watch them and see that it works, are in the process of finding a common struggle, and that's precisely what humanity has lacked since the dawn of time: a common cause, that is to say, one that goes beyond current cleavages: "We want to institute for ourselves the political power we lack."

In a people that has become constitutive, and therefore vigilant, there is no room for tyrants.

From the same author

Writing the Constitution, workbook of the Yellow Vests
Constituents, Talma Studios Publishing, 2019

The links

To continue working, you will find many resources
on the Internet, and I recommend in particular:

http://etienne.chouard.free.fr/Europe/precieuses_pepites.pdf
http://wiki.gentilsvirus.org/index.php/Accueil
http://lavraiedemocratie.fr/
https://www.article3.fr/
http://www.le-message.org/

Table of contents

8. Conclusion
The nice surprise of Christmas 2018:
the "yellow vests" show us the way 91

From the same author

The links